# Blacksmithing

José Antonio Ares

LARK
BOOKS

A Division of Sterling Publishing Co., Inc.
New York / London

Library of Congress Cataloging-in-Publication Data

Ares, José Antonio.
  [Forja. English]
  Blacksmithing : hot techniques & striking projects / José Antonio Ares.
--1st ed.
      p. cm.
  Includes index.
  ISBN 978-1-60059-384-0 (PB with flaps : alk. paper)
  1.  Blacksmithing.  I. Title.
  TT220.A7413 2008
  682--dc22

                                    2008020202

10 9 8 7 6 5 4 3 2 1

First Edition

Published by Lark Books
A Division of Sterling Publishing Co., Inc.
387 Park Avenue South, New York, NY 10016

English Translation © 2008, Lark Books

Distributed in Canada by Sterling Publishing,
c/o Canadian Manda Group, 165 Dufferin Street
Toronto, Ontario, Canada M6K 3H6

Distributed in the United Kingdom by GMC Distribution Services,
Castle Place, 166 High Street, Lewes, East Sussex, England BN7 1XU

Distributed in Australia by Capricorn Link (Australia) Pty Ltd.,
P.O. Box 704, Windsor, NSW 2756 Australia

If you have questions or comments about this book,
please contact:
Lark Books, 67 Broadway, Asheville, NC 28801
828-253-0467

ISBN 13: 978-1-60059-384-0

Project and production: Parramon Ediciones, S.A.

Text: José Antonio Ares
Projects: José Antonio Ares, Ernest Altés
Photographs: Nos & Soto, Ernest Altés, Ares, Museu Cau Ferrat
Illustrations: Farrés il-lustració editorial
Translated from Spanish by Eric A. Bye, M.A.

1st edition: September, 2007
© 2007 Parramon Ediciones, S.A. -  Exclusive publishing
rights  Worldwide
Ronda de Sant Pere, 5, 4th floor
08010 Barcelona, Spain

Subsidiary of the Norma Publishing Group
of Latin America
© of authorized reproductions, VEGAP,
Barcelona, 2007
www.parramon.com
ISBN: 978-84-342-3205-1
Legal deposit: B-42.254-2007
Printed in Spain

# Blacksmithing

# Materials
## and tools

# Techniques

# Step by step

introd

This book presents traditional and modern blacksmithing methods. It covers classic skills, such as punching and twisting, and contemporary techniques, such as plasma cutting, heating with a torch, and using electric tools. The goal of this book is to combine ancient practices with current technological advances so that you can take creative advantage of all available resources.

The skills in the Basic Techniques chapter and the projects in the Step by Step chapter were selected so that one person, working alone, could complete them. This approach makes it simple to enter the world of artistic blacksmithing.

Many blacksmiths make their own tools based on the requirements of their projects. In the tools chapter, we have attempted to describe only those required for the skill without presenting an extensive catalog of all of the tools available to purchase or to make.

uction

We will be working exclusively with carbon steel as a forging material so from this point on, to facilitate quick and thorough learning, we will refer to carbon steel simply as steel. We intentionally omitted other materials, such as copper, aluminum, and stainless steel, because forging these metals requires a more advanced skill set.

Finally, a photo gallery of artworks by well-known as well as anonymous smiths shows the creative possibilities of the forge.

We encourage you to get involved, to use the different techniques presented to gain skill and knowledge, and to experiment without hesitation.

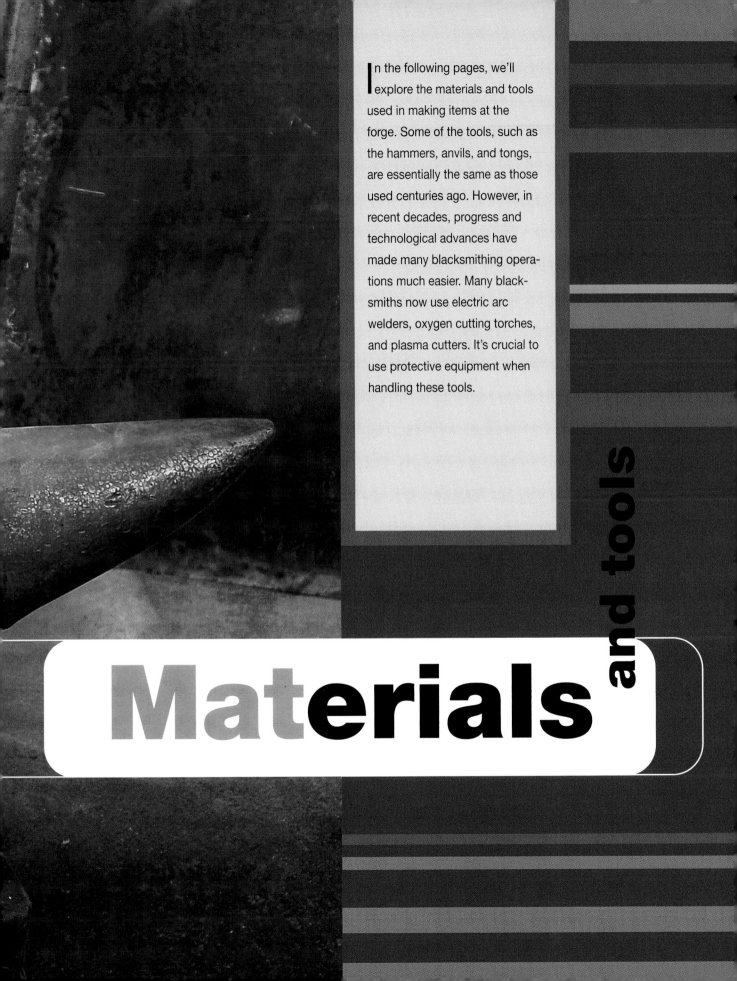

In the following pages, we'll explore the materials and tools used in making items at the forge. Some of the tools, such as the hammers, anvils, and tongs, are essentially the same as those used centuries ago. However, in recent decades, progress and technological advances have made many blacksmithing operations much easier. Many blacksmiths now use electric arc welders, oxygen cutting torches, and plasma cutters. It's crucial to use protective equipment when handling these tools.

# Materials and tools

# RAW MATERIALS

## iron and **steel**

### CHARACTERISTICS

The best raw material for the black-smithing shop is steel, specifically mild steel. It's the easiest to shape using blacksmithing techniques such as hammering.

Sometimes, steel is also called iron, but this is technically a misnomer. Iron is an element with less than 0.05 percentage of carbon. It's very soft and can be hammered but not hardened. Steel is an alloy of iron and carbon. The amount of carbon dictates both the hardness of the steel and its elasticity so that it can en-

dure heat-treating such as tempering. If the iron contains a percentage of carbon over 1.7, it's fragile and breakable. Because it isn't ductile and malleable, it must be melted. This material is commonly used in mold casting because of its great fusibility. Steel worked in a forging process must be easy to shape and

capable of stretching through hammering to form rods, some very fine, without breaking or cracking. The carbon content must be around 0.15 percent so that the steel is not too hard or too soft.

Typical cast doorknocker in the shape of a hand holding a ball. Casting is commonly used for making pieces in special molds.

Steel can be shaped after heating it in the forge and striking it with a hammer.

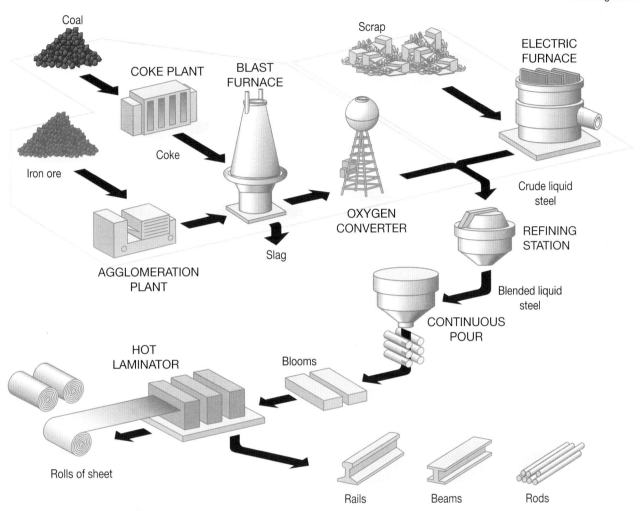

Coal

COKE PLANT

Coke

Iron ore

AGGLOMERATION PLANT

BLAST FURNACE

Slag

OXYGEN CONVERTER

Scrap

ELECTRIC FURNACE

Crude liquid steel

REFINING STATION

Blended liquid steel

CONTINUOUS POUR

HOT LAMINATOR

Blooms

Rolls of sheet

Rails      Beams      Rods

## STEEL MANUFACTURING

Steel is produced from iron ore and scrap.

Blast furnaces refine the pig iron (iron ore) into quality steel by forcing high-pressure oxygen through the melted metal.

The oxygen combines with the carbon and the undesirable elements to initiate a high temperature oxidation reaction that burns out the impurities of the pig iron.

At the same time, fluxes such as lime are added to create a chemical reaction that generates heat (around 3000°F/1650°C). When the proper composition for steel is achieved, it's poured into the continuous pour vat. This process can produce up to 300 tons of steel in just an hour. Electric furnaces are used to manufacture special steels and stainless steels because they don't use fuels that cause impurities. The scrap must first be analyzed and classified because its alloy content will affect the composition of the refined metal. Electric furnaces make it possible to control the temperature with great precision. A voltaic arc is generated between two large electrodes inside a hermetically sealed chamber of the furnace. This produces 3500°F (1930°C) of heat for melting the load of metal. The precise quantities of the needed alloy materials are then added.

*Materials and tools*

11

Various tubes manufactured cold
from sheets of different thicknesses

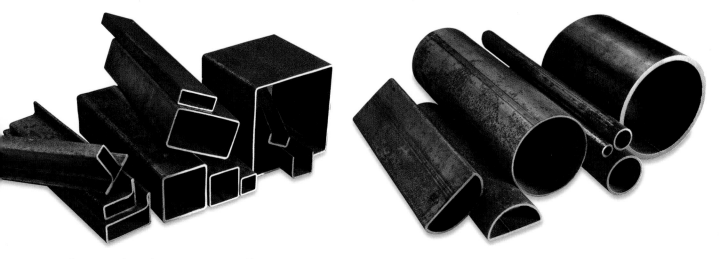

# introducing **metals**

There are a great number of finished
steel products on the market. Sheets and
bars come in a wide variety of thicknesses and cross-sections. These products
are conveniently standardized based on
their shape, finish, and ultimate use, and
are produced through cold forming or
heat lamination.

## COLD FORMING

Cold-formed steel shapes are made from
a fine sheet ($\frac{1}{32}$ to $\frac{1}{4}$ inch [1 to 6 mm] in
thickness) used in shapers that bend and
fold the metal at ambient temperature.
The sheet is bent and folded in various
rollers until it takes on the complex
shape of the desired profile. The various

profiles are then joined through arc
welding. This is commonly used in
constructing furniture, metal handrails,
and frames for doors and windows.

Basic outline of the phases of
manufacturing a round tube in
an automatic shaper

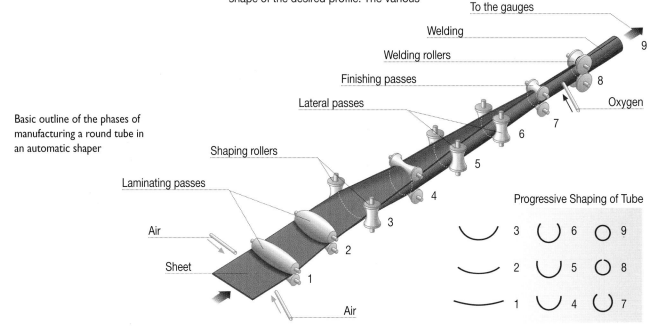

Progressive Shaping of Tube

Various shapes produced by hot laminating

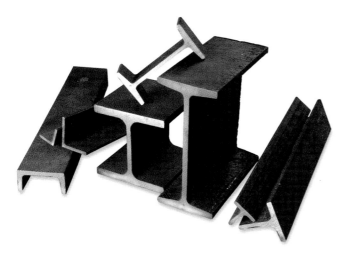

## HOT LAMINATING

In hot laminating, the temperature of the metal is raised to around 2200°F (1200°C) and then passed between two rollers located one above the other and turning in opposite directions. During this process, the metal is subjected to tremendous pressure, which changes its structure. This creates a continual forging effect that improves the characteristics of the material. It eliminates any trace of weld or impurities that may have been produced in melting and increases the ductility and resilience of the metal. It becomes more resistant to breaking through traction, compression, or torsion.

Because of their mechanical properties (elastic behavior), these shapes are most often used in civil engineering construction such as bridges, high-tension cable towers, in the marine industry, and for the structure of buildings.

Diagram of the basic function of a laminator

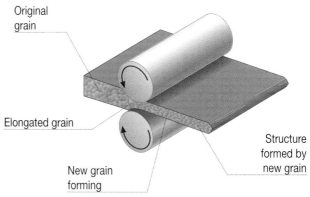

Original grain

Elongated grain

New grain forming

Structure formed by new grain

Many functional works are made by forging and combining different shapes that are available commercially. *Hercules Fountain* (47 x 20 x 20 inches [120 x 50 x 50 cm]) by Antoni Gaudí, Gardens of the Pedralbes Palace (Barcelona, Spain).

# FUELS

Charcoal

Various fuels generate the heat necessary to bring metals to the proper forging temperature. They made be solid, like coal. Liquid fuels, including diesel, are also used, as are gaseous fuels, including oxygen, propane, and acetylene. In this book we will deal only with the most common fuels used in a blacksmith shop: coal, acetylene, and propane.

## Coal

The coal most commonly used is soft and crushed to pieces roughly the size of an almond. The coal is moistened with water so that it forms a compact vault or cave in the hearth of the forge where high temperatures can be reached and maintained. This cuts down on the time needed to heat the metal. Sometimes, charcoal, made from carbonized hardwoods such as oak and holm oak, is used for fuel. It's most often used for special projects where careful temperature control may be needed, such as in creating light alloys at a low fusion temperature. Other types of coal, such as coke, anthracite, and lignite are less commonly used. Anthracite is very expensive and lignite has a limited heating capacity.

Soft coal

Coal arch produced by sprinkling the hot coals with water.

Flame temperature

| | |
|---|---|
| 6152°F | |
| 5792°F | 5792°F/3200°C (Acetylene) |
| 5432°F | 5162°F/2850°C (Propane) |
| 5072°F | 5018°F/2770°C (Natural Gas) |
| 4712°F | |
| 4352°F | |
| 3992°F | |
| 3632°F | |

Acetylene    Propane    Natural Gas

Comparison of flame temperatures produced by mixing oxygen with various gases

Storage tanks for oxygen (black) and acetylene (red)

# Gases

Acetylene and propane are the most commonly used gasses in blacksmithing shops. These are sold in high-pressure metal cylinders either painted in colors recognized internationally or labeled for identification.

A mix of welding torch oxygen and acetylene or oxygen and propane are most commonly used to produce a flame that reaches a high temperature. It's also possible to combine oxygen and domestic piped-in gas, but the resulting temperature won't be as high. The flame is generally used to localize and limit the heating on the metal to be forged so that specific bends, twists, accents, and up-sets can be produced without having to work the piece in the fire of the forge. Using a flame in this way also prevents inadequate heating that could cause other parts of the piece to warp.

Localized heating with an oxygen and propane torch

Storage tanks for oxygen (black) and propane (orange)

# PROTECTIVE MATERIALS

Tools and products for producing a black patina: gas torch, linseed oil, and wax

## patinas

Metals must be given a patina (varnish, wax, or paint) to protect them from rust.

Applied with a cotton cloth or brush to the surface of a metal object, this coating gives it a finish that appears aged. Before applying a patina, the metal should be cleaned of oils and any vestiges of rust. The easiest patina consists of a mixture of distilled water and salt. As time goes by, this mixture produces a layer of rust that protects the metal. Ultimately, it must be fixed by applying a varnish to form a thin, hard coating on the metal.

**Black finish patina:** This is applied to forged pieces and conserves the texture produced by working them on the anvil. Linseed oil is applied, and then the piece is heated in the gas flame of a torch to produce the proper blackening. After the metal has completely cooled, it's rubbed with a cotton cloth and wax to seal the pores.

**Graphite patina:** This is used to produce a gray protective patina. The graphite is diluted in linseed oil to create a homogenous paste. A universal solvent is then added to it. Various pigments can be added to darken or color the patina.

**Varnishes:** These form a thin, hard, transparent coating on the metal. The finish is shiny and lustrous, unifying the surface colors.

**Waxes:** Like varnishes, wax is used to polish and unify the surface of an object. The desired shine is achieved through applying the wax with a cotton cloth and then rubbing with more or less energy.

**Gum lacquer varnish:** This is a well-mixed combination of 5¼ ounces (150 g) of gum lacquer scales and a quart/liter of denatured alcohol.

**Paints:** Paints are prepared by mixing pigments and colorings with synthetic binders. They adhere well to the metal and can have an opaque, glossy, or matte finish.

Gum lacquer scales and denatured alcohol for making gum lacquer varnish

Graphite patina made from linseed oil, graphite, black pigment, and universal solvent

# preparing varnish
## to protect metal

A layer of rosin and wax is applied with a brush to protect metal from rust. It also evens out the colors and, when dry, provides a satiny sheen for easier application of the final finish.

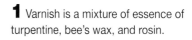

**1** Varnish is a mixture of essence of turpentine, bee's wax, and rosin.

**2** Bee's wax sheets are cut into pieces so it will dissolve more easily.

**3** Crystallized hunks of rosin are dissolved by wrapping them in a cloth and pulverizing them with a hammer.

**4** Mix by weight one part bee's wax and one part rosin in an enamel container. Add three parts essence of turpentine and dissolve the mixture in a double boiler, producing a liquid.

**5** The mixture thickens into a semi-liquid product as it cools.

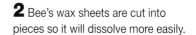

*Materials and tools*

17

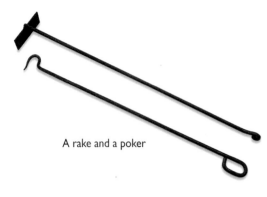

A rake and a poker

# BASIC TOOLS

## the **forge**

### PARTS OF THE FORGE

The forge has three pieces: a base, a fan, and a hood. The base, also known as the hearth, is where the coal is burned and the pieces of metal are heated. It's placed at a certain height above the floor and covered with refractory brick. The fan, operated by electric motor, is usually located beneath the hearth. It provides a regular supply of air to intensify the fire. The exhaust hood vents the smoke and gases through a chimney.

The coal bin is sometimes located next to the forge. More often, it's stored outdoors to make better use of the workspace. A complete set of forge equipment includes a poker for rearranging the hot coals and a container of water to sprinkle onto the coal or to cool the pieces that have been heated.

Old forge with bellows

Complete forge setup

Fan and ducts connecting to the base of the forge

Portable forge

1

# **lighting** the forge

Next, we will present one of the various methods of lighting the forge; this is not the only way, and different people use different methods.

Once the fire is lit, wait until the sulfurous gases that the coal gives off are consumed before heating the steel, as they could harm it.

**1** Before lighting the forge, check and clean the air supply duct for the fan to be sure that there are no left-over coals or ashes. Place coal in the hearth of the forge. Using the poker, open up a space in the center of the base just above the air outlet to facilitate air delivery from the fan and ignition of the fire.

**2** Kindle the fire in the middle of the opening using paper and wood shavings, and light with a match, cigarette lighter, or another convenient lighter.

**3** Gradually, use the fan to supply air to the fire through the vent. At the same time, add coal to the fire.

2

3

4

**4** A column of dense smoke indicates that the coal has caught. Because the smoke contains sulfurous compounds that can damage the metal, don't put the steel into the hot coals until this smoke has burned off.

**5** The fire is at the right point for heating pieces. To avoid rust formation on the steel, don't place it right above the air vent.

5

*Materials and tools*

# **color** and temperature

## GENERAL INFORMATION

Metal is heated with a view toward its mass and its physical and chemical characteristics.

Metal heated without following the proper steps is at risk. Essential characteristics, such as reducing resistance to rust, may be changed in the process. The speed of the heating depends on:

– the physical and chemical nature of the metal. A metal that conducts heat better than another will take on heat more quickly.

– the mass and the relationship among its dimensions. Pieces with a greater surface area will absorb more calories and heat up more quickly, even if it weighs the same or is made out of the same material as another piece.

– the temperature of the coals in the forge.

In the half-light of a darkened area, it's easier to judge the shades metal passes through as it is heated in the forge.

## COLOR AND TEMPERATURE

Heating metal produces color changes that vary according to the temperature and thereby help to identify it. For example, dark cherry red indicates that the temperature is up to about 1562°F (850°C), and orange equates to about 1832°F (1000°C). Judging the color depends on the composition of the steel and the light in which it is examined. In order to see the shades of the heated steel, it's advisable to inspect them in the half-light of a darkened area.

Pieces should be heated in moderation and occasionally turned in the hot coals. This encourages even heating of all surfaces and heats the heart of the piece, especially important for thick cross sections. The piece should be placed in the coals far enough from the direct air intake through the vent to prevent surface oxidation but deep enough in the coals so that it doesn't get too hot in the reduction area.

Relation between color and temperature in heated steel

2552°F (1400°C) Pale white upper lim forged ste

2372°F (1300°C) white yell

2192°F (1200°C) pale yello

2012°F (1100°C) yellow

1832°F (1000°C) orange

1742°F (950°C) yellowish red

1652°F (900°C) light red

1562°F (850°C) red

1490°F (810°C) light cherry red
1472°F (800°C)

1400°F (760°C) cherry red
1364°F (740°C) dark cherry red

1292°F (700°C) Minimum for temperature
1256° (680°C) dark red

1148°F (620°C) brownish red
1112°F (600°C)

1022°F (550°C) dark brown

932°F (500°C)

752°F (400°C)

680°F (360°C) gray
644°F (340°C) bluish gray
608°F (320°C) light blue
572°F (300°C) blue
554°F (290°C) dark blue
536°F (280°C) purple
518°F (270°C) reddish purple
500°F (260°C) bronze
482°F (250°C) brown
464°F (240°C) dark straw
446°F (230°C) light yellow
428°F (220°C) straw
392°F (200°C) light yellow

Examples of
blacksmith's tongs

# tongs

Tongs are a basic tool for black-smithing made from two articulated bars and a hinge that separates them into the handles, by which they are held, and the jaws. The jaws, used to secure the pieces as they are worked, come in various configurations to be more useful with differently shaped metal. The jaws may be flat, rounded, grooved, L-shaped, squared, and so forth. Tongs are used to insert, manipulate, turn, and remove pieces from the hot coals. They help to prevent working too close to the fire and inadvertently touching the hot steel, and are especially useful for heating small pieces.

Heat can warp the tongs and hard usage can open the jaws to an ineffective point. They require periodic maintenance to assure a good, safe grip on the shape of steel being worked.

Tong jaws working
with metal

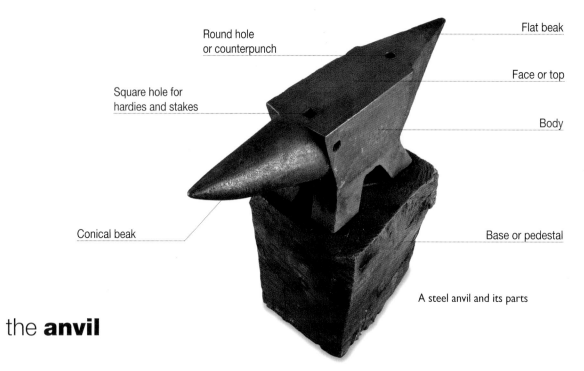

Round hole
or counterpunch

Square hole for
hardies and stakes

Conical beak

Flat beak

Face or top

Body

Base or pedestal

A steel anvil and its parts

# the **anvil**

The tool par excellence for the blacksmith shop is made from a block of solid forged steel, where metal is forged with hammer blows. The anvil generally weighs from 75 to 440 pounds (34 to 200 kg), depending on the work for which it is intended. The top surface of the anvil usually has a couple of holes—a square one to accommodate forging accessories, and another rounded one, which is referred to as a

counterpunch or pritchel hole. This is used for punching holes and making bends. The anvil typically has one or two characteristic points known as beaks, one conical and the other flat or pyramid-shaped. These are used for stretching, bending, and folding operations. Anvils are placed onto sturdy, very stable bases, commonly of oak, which absorb the blows and reduce the rebound effect. The height of the anvil top

should enable the blacksmith to keep his back almost straight while working and should reach the knuckles of the standing blacksmith's hands.

The anvil must be near the forge so that the blacksmith can be located between the two, take the heated steel out of the hearth, and turn immediately to the anvil to work with it.

Forging on the flat beak of the anvil

Forging on the conical beak of the anvil

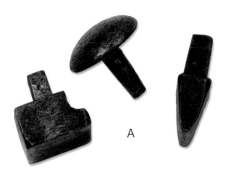

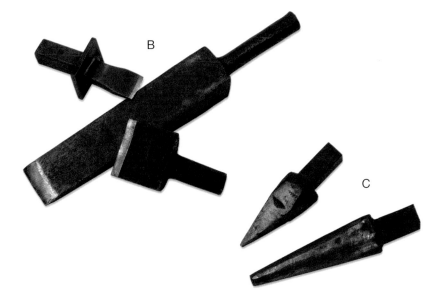

Stakes (A), hardies (B), and
forging cones (C)

## ADDITIONAL TOOLS FOR THE ANVIL

Sometimes, additional tools for the anvil are needed for delicate or special blacksmithing projects. They're used in forging pieces or parts that are either cold or hot. These accessories have a square peg on the bottom that fits into the square hole in the anvil to keep the tool from turning or moving in use.

Many of these accessories are made by the blacksmith to meet the requirements of a particular work. Some are so specialized that they are discarded or recycled after being used one time.

**Stakes:** make it possible to hammer the steel and bend it, flatten it, or groove it.

**Hardies:** are used for cutting steel pieces, either hot or cold. They fit into the square hardy hole with a cutting edge facing upwards. Metal is held on top of the cutting edge and then struck with a hammer.

**Bending tool:** is used for bending and curving steel on the anvil.

**Forging cones:** are used for bending hoops or rings and for curved or square pieces.

Bending tool

Bending a heated strap
in a bending tool

Locking pliers and a manual screw clamp

Various forging hammers

# Blacksmith **Hammers and Clamps**

**Ball and Peen Hammers:** are essential in forging work with cold or hot metal. The most common types are ball hammers with a nearly spherical ball on one end, and the peens, which have a rounded face. Their weight varies between roughly 2 pounds and 4½ pounds (.9 and 2 kg), depending on the type of work being done.

**Blacksmith's Vise:** is the most commonly used holding device in forging work. This is a solid tool made of forged, tempered steel to withstand great pressures. It consists of a movable jaw held away from a fixed jaw by a laminated spring. Normally, blacksmith vises are attached to the legs of a workbench using screws and clamps. Sometimes, special arrangements are made for their installation to free up space and make it easier to work on large pieces.

**Bench Vises:** are made of either cast or forged steel. Vises are used to hold pieces firmly so they can be filed, cut, bent, or perforated, among other operations.

**Hand Vises:** make it possible to hold pieces of different thickness. Their portability makes them essential in the blacksmith's shop.

**Locking Pliers:** are very practical for working on pieces that are difficult to hold because of their small size. Locking pliers exert pressure by adjusting the opening between the jaws to the thickness of the piece.

Blacksmith vises

Bench vise

Bending tools

Forks

Punches

# More Blacksmith **Tools**

**Bending Tools:** are used as levers on steel forms to bend, fold, or twist them. The blacksmith makes them based on the shape he needs to create.

**Bending Forks:** are U-shaped tools made by the blacksmith to impart a curve of a certain radius. They can be made from round bar stock bent into a U shape or simply two pieces of the same bar welded to a base.

**Punches:** are made from round or square rods of hard steel with a sharpened point on one end. They make holes

in red-hot metals as the punch is struck on the other end with a hammer.

**Templates for Curves:** are tools used for reproducing the same shape several times. The blacksmith makes them from sheet stock with the desired shape welded onto a steel base.

**Nail Heading Tool:** is a tool for making forged nails and rivets with round or square holes of various sizes. Commonly made by blacksmiths, they're used over the round hole in the top of the anvil.

**Rivet Set and Base Plate:** are tools used to shape the heads of rivets. The rivet set is round in cross section and has a hardened and tempered opening in the rear. The mouth has a semicircular opening where the heads of the rivets are placed for swaging (tapering) to shape. The base plate is placed into the square hole of the anvil. The head of the previously forged rivet is placed on it so that it won't be distorted while the other end is being formed.

Template for curves

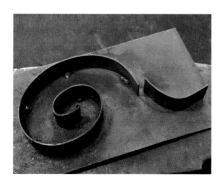

Nail headers

Rivet sets and base

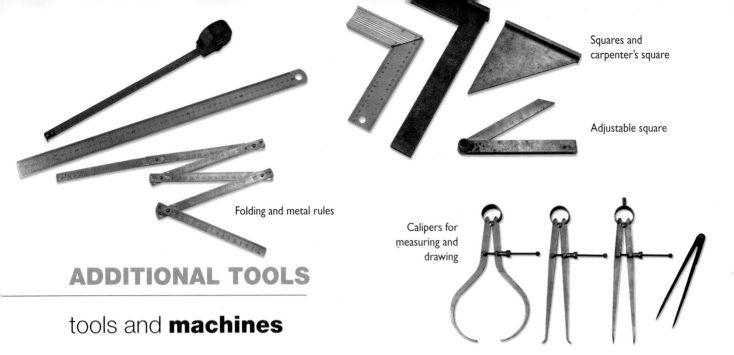

Squares and carpenter's square

Adjustable square

Folding and metal rules

Calipers for measuring and drawing

## ADDITIONAL TOOLS

## tools and **machines**

On the following pages, we'll describe the additional tools and machines used for cutting, perforating, and welding steel. In addition, measuring, tracing, and marking tools will round out the workshop inventory for the usual forging jobs.

**Metal and Folding Rules:** are made of stainless steel and very helpful for drawing lines on metals. A folding rule is a strip of thin, flexible steel used to measure flat surfaces and large objects. Rules commonly come in lengths of 3 to 16½ feet or more (1 to 5 meters), in contrast to measuring tapes, which are used for measuring lengths over 30 feet (10 meters).

**Squares and Adjustable Squares:** are used for marking and checking right angles. Never check a large surface with a small square because possible errors aren't visible beyond the end of the tool. The adjustable square is useful for transferring and marking certain angles, and for checking and confirming them. It consists of two jointed pieces that facilitate drawing any angle.

**Calipers and Compasses:** are made of steel and fitted with hardened ends, and are either simple or spring-operated. In addition to drawing arcs, compasses are very useful for transferring measurements during forging work. Measuring

compasses, which have either concave or convex arms, are used for comparing and checking the exterior or interior of pieces and objects.

**Center Punch:** is a steel tool with a hardened and tempered point that's used for marking guide points for drawing arcs and circumferences. It's also used to mark the center that will guide a drill bit.

**Scribe or Scratch Awl:** is a steel rod with a very sharp, hardened point. It's used to mark straight lines with the help of metal rules and squares.

Center punches

Scribes

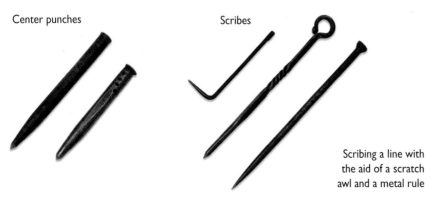

Scribing a line with the aid of a scratch awl and a metal rule

Cross sections of files: triangular (A), flat (B), square (C), knife (D), round (E), and half-round (F)

Different types of files

**Files:** are used to remove rough, cut edges and to smooth out surfaces. Files are distinguished by their shape, length, and coarseness (fine or coarse). Files are slid, under pressure, across a surface or along an edge.

**Frame Saws:** are tools composed of a steel frame or bow that holds and tightens a saw blade. Two clamps, one at each end of the bow, control the tension on the blade.

**Chisels:** are also referred to as cold chisels. They're wedge-shaped cutting instruments made of hard steel with a tempered edge.

**Burins:** have a tapered cutting edge that runs at an angle to the body. They are used for making grooves and flutes.

**Mechanical Shear:** is a sturdy tool that is used in cutting flat shapes of various thickness. Some are capable of cutting T- or L-shaped stock.

The lever operates the shear and the gearing multiplies the force exerted on it. The longer the lever, the greater the force.

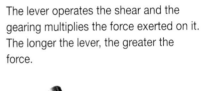

Burins and chisels

Frame saws

Mechanical shear

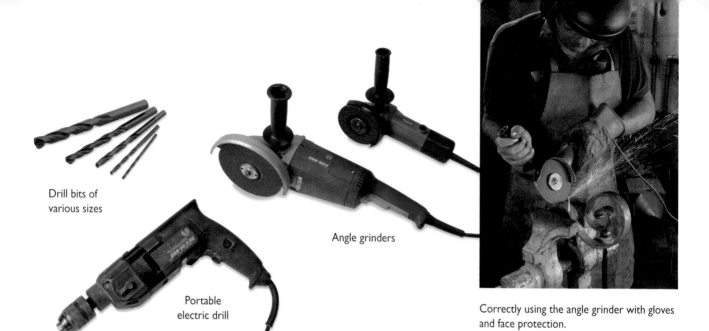

Drill bits of various sizes

Angle grinders

Portable electric drill

Correctly using the angle grinder with gloves and face protection.

**Portable Electric Drill:** This is an electric motor that imparts a continuous rotation to the chuck, which secures the drill bits.

**Drill Bits:** are cylindrical rods of hardened and tempered steel in varying diameters. They have spiral flutes with a cutting edge that start at their tip. The harder and more durable the material to be drilled, the greater the angle required on the tip.

**Angle Grinder:** is a portable electric tool that functions at a high rpm (rotations per minute) of 6,000 to 10,000 as it spins abrasive disks. The disks get worn down as they cut or abrade and produce filings in the form of sparks.

**Jigsaw:** is portable and electric and used for quickly doing straight or curved open work. The electric motor imparts an elliptical movement to a saw blade attached to a movable axle.

**Band Saw:** is an electric bench tool with a continuous saw blade that produces a continuous cut. It has adjustable speeds for handling different metals and can produce 90° to 45° angle cuts.

**Electric Bench Grinder:** is a machine tool used for sharpening tools and removing rough edges through abrasion. It has an electric motor and abrasive wheels at each end, usually one each of fine and coarse grits.

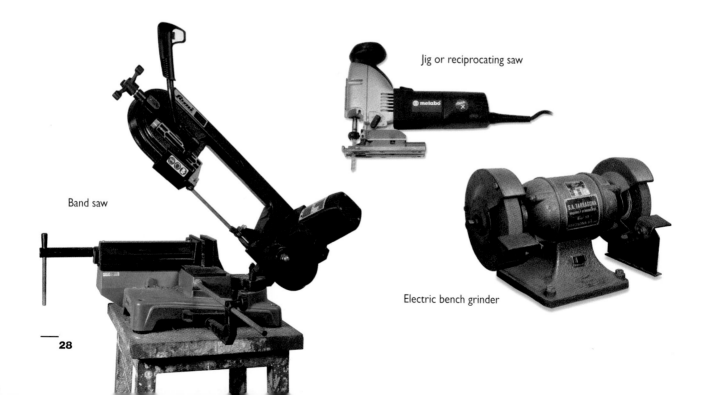

Jig or reciprocating saw

Band saw

Electric bench grinder

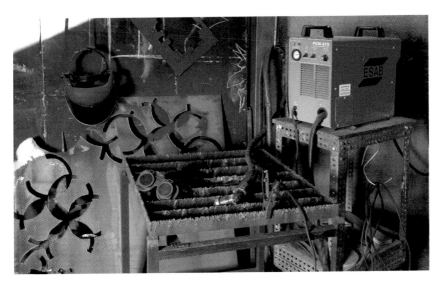

Oxyacetylene welding equipment

Plasma cutting
equipment

**Plasma Cutting Equipment:** involves a high-frequency generator that produces an electric arc between the nozzle located on the torch and the ground clamp. A gauge on the front measures the outlet for the air necessary for plasma formation. It also has a control for the current output, which is adjustable from 10 to 60 amps.

**Oxygen Cutting Equipment:** has two tanks containing pressurized gases (acetylene, propane, and oxygen) and two manometers indicating and maintaining ideal working gas pressure. A cutting torch mixes the gases and combusts and removes the steel.

**Oxyacetylene Welding Torch:** also has two tanks that contain pressurized gas. However, the torch is different from that of the oxygen cutting equipment. Its nozzle is designed for joining steel by melting it.

**Welding Equipment with Coated Rod:** is an electric welding device. A transformer modifies the electric energy from the distribution network into either an alternating or a direct current at lower tension. This device combines the electrode clip and the ground clip to make the welding circuit.

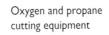

Oxygen and propane
cutting equipment

Welder for coated rod
and protective shield

Metal hooks hung on the wall store bar stock until it is used.

# general **safety** considerations

### SHOP ORGANIZATION

The blacksmith's shop needs to be an efficient, creative area where it is possible to work comfortably and without danger from the materials, machines, and tools.

By observing a few sensible rules of neatness and safety, the best possible work environment can be created and accidents avoided.

Commonly used tools, such as hammers, tongs, and electric tools, must be kept in specially designated places (on holders and in cabinets) that make it easy to use them, and where they are returned after they have been used.

Cut-offs and work scraps should be kept in containers so they can be reused or recycled in subsequent projects. A storage place solely for storing shapes that are likely to be used in new jobs is important, as is the avoidance of compulsive storage. Keep only the things that will be used for projects in the foreseeable future.

A metal receptacle made by the blacksmith serves as storage for leftover pieces from finished projects.

It's best to discard hammers with a damaged striking surface to prevent pieces of metal from flying off and causing serious injuries.

Ear muffs and foam plugs

Basic personal protection equipment for a black-smith's shop

## PERSONAL PROTECTION ITEMS

Personal protection is one of the most important safety features in the workshop. Rotary grinders, electric saws, oxygen torches, and plasma cutters all produce shavings or red-hot particles during cutting or polishing, welding, grinding, or pounding hot steel on the anvil.

A leather apron, protective gloves, and glasses keep any particles from coming into contact with the body. Avoid burns by wearing leather gloves while welding, grinding, and cutting with an oxygen torch. Safety shoes protect the feet from accidental blows.

It's a good idea to use earmuffs or foam plugs to deaden the noise of the hammer on the anvil and from tools in general.

In this chapter we will explain the basic, traditional techniques of blacksmithing, along with some others that are relatively new, such as cutting with oxygen and a stream of plasma. Combining traditional techniques with new technological advances facilitates the creation of forged items without losing creativity. We've chosen techniques that can be used by a person working alone, which will make it easier to become familiar with them.

basic Techniques

# BASIC CONSIDERATIONS

These most common, basic techniques are grouped according to the effect they produce in the metal. We have also included a section on welding techniques, since they are an inseparable part of any blacksmith shop, no matter how modest. Any can be done without the help of another person in the forging process, and all require continuous practice.

## techniques for **section changes**

Techniques that enlarge, reduce, or modify the original section of a commercially produced shape include upsetting, drawing out, tapering, laminating, and forging nails.

### Upsetting

The purpose of upsetting is to broaden and shorten the end of the steel for making such things as nail heads and ball-shaped ends on bars.

To upset a piece properly, the area to be broadened is heated to light orange. The heat must be even and extend to the center of the steel. At the same time, it's necessary to sprinkle water on the part of the rod that is not going to be upset; that way it will not bend under the hammer blows. Still, it's normal for the bar to bend a little just above the flared area. This must be controlled and corrected during the whole process.

Once the piece is heated, it's struck in a direction parallel to the steel that is to be upset. The blows can be dealt in different ways based on the thickness and the length of the piece. The heated area of the bar can be hammered on the anvil, held in the blacksmith's vise, or struck right on the face of the anvil. The upsetting is usually repeated several times.

Upsetting the head of a rivet on the blacksmith's vise. Here, the end of the shaft is hammered as it's heated by the torch (left).

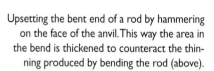

Upsetting the bent end of a rod by hammering on the face of the anvil. This way the area in the bend is thickened to counteract the thinning produced by bending the rod (above).

Another way to upset the steel is to strike the heated bar directly onto the face of the anvil (left).

## DRAWING OUT A TENON

Next we show the process of stretching a rod on just one side.

**1** To begin drawing out the steel, place the appropriately heated rod on the edge of the anvil face, and strike it. This forces the material to displace and marks the start of the stretching.

**1**

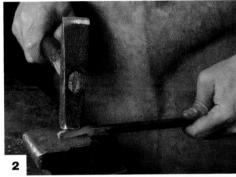
**2**

**3**

Sequence of the drawing-out process using a tenon

## Drawing Out

The process of drawing out involves lengthening the material at the same time the thickness is reduced. To achieve this, the area to be drawn out is heated to a bright red and hammered, either on some part of the anvil such as the round horn or the face, or on a hardy. The drawing out is usually done in several phases, so as the steel stretches and thins, be careful to avoid heating it too much and ruining it in the hot coals.

**2** Continue drawing out the steel on a flat hardy by striking the heated end with a hammer. Repeat this operation to produce the desired stretching.

**3** Heat the drawn-out end very carefully to apply the finishing touches.

Detail of a gate finial made by Antoni Gaudí at the Güell Winery.

*Basic techniques*

35

## Tapering

Tapering finishes off the section of the commercially supplied shape to a point or a thin line. This reduces the initial section while simultaneously producing a lengthening in the material. To achieve this, heat the steel to bright red, and hammer it on the face of the anvil. Repeat the operation several times, if necessary, taking special care in heating the tapered point.

Process of tapering a square rod

Detail of tapers made by Antoni Gaudí on the entry to the Güell Winery

## Laminating

Laminating reduces the initial section by hammering out the material to increase its width. The piece must be heated in proportion to its thickness, keeping in mind that it will be easier to flatten if the temperature is higher. Thus, the hammering out is best done with the steel at light yellow rather than dark red.

Process of laminating a round rod

Sequence in the process of laminating a round rod. Note that the operation of hammering out is done in various stages to ensure the right temperature for working the steel.

Modern door knocker in the Gracia neighborhood of Barcelona, Spain. The impression of the natural leaf is created through laminating.

# Forging Nails

Forged nails are created through a combination of basic techniques including upsetting, laminating, tapering, and trimming, among others. A manual heading tool with a handle and one or more holes in the shapes and sizes appropriate for the nails are required. In general terms, this process involves drawing out and tapering the rod to create the shaft of the nail and trimming it on a hardy attached to the anvil. The head of the nail is created through upsetting in the heading tool. The piece is heated several times during the forging process.

### MAKING A NAIL
The following sequence begins with the end of the nail previously hammered out and tapered, as demonstrated in previous pages.

Tapered, trimmed, upset, and shaped; the sequence for making a nail

**1** A heated rod, tapered in advance, is struck gently on a hardy in the anvil to mark the end where the nail will be cut or trimmed.

Renaissance nail on the entrance door to the Church of Santa Maria la Major in the town of Prades, Spain

**2** The rod is then inserted into the hole in the heading tool held over the round hole on the face of the anvil. It's bent over until it breaks free where the cut was marked on the hardy.

**3** The head of the nail is upset on the heading tool by shaping the steel at bright red heat.

**4** The nail is then held with appropriate tongs and is worked and shaped using the hammer.

Basic techniques

37

This section brings together such techniques as rolling and making clips and spiral scrolls, among others. All are variations on the curving and bending processes. These are very expressive techniques commonly used in making forged items. Some can be worked cold without having to heat the steel, as long as the thickness of the material allows it. Still, for the best results, it's usually necessary to use heat.

## Cold Bending and Twisting

There is no heat involved in cold bending and twisting the steel. Usually, the process is limited by the thickness of the piece. Bending involves imparting a curve, and twisting creates a spiral in the steel. The blacksmith uses tools that multiply force such as bending forks, hand bending tools, and various tools for clamping both to the face of the anvil and the blacksmith's vise. Curves and twists can also be done with cold steel by hammering on the rounded anvil beak or right on the blacksmith's vise.

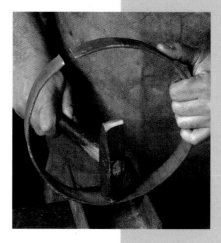

Using a U-shaped form on the anvil face to bend a piece of strap. The hammering bends the strap at the point located between the ends of the shape.

The process of bending the strap on the rounded anvil

Bending in a fork held between the jaws of the blacksmith's vise. In this case, a bending tool is used for better control of the curve.

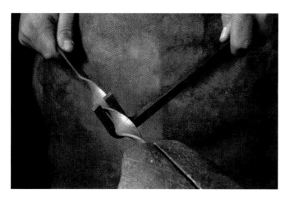

Using a bending tool to cold bend a strap

Detail of a grate entirely made through cold bending by Ares

## Hot Bending and Twisting

Heating the steel to temperature facilitates and simplifies the forging process and achieves the greatest plasticity. The metal must be heated to bright red through to the center to avoid possible cracks during the bending. Just as with the cold processes, bending tools, forks, and auxiliary anvil tools are used to make the curves and twists. Tongs are often used to manipulate the heated steel.

Detail of bends and twists created through heat; entrance to the Güell Winery by Antoni Gaudí

Hot bending a square rod on a bending fork clamped in the blacksmith's vise, using appropriate tongs for safety

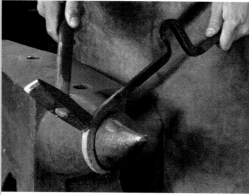

Curving the end of a piece on the round anvil horn

Using tongs to bend a strap into a spiral shape on a special template

Hot twisting a rod in the blacksmith's vise with the help of a hand-bending tool. The rod was flattened in advance in the area to be twisted.

# Rolling

Rolling involves bending the steel onto itself to create spirals and scrolls. Hammer the heated end directly on the face of the anvil to make a small curve, and continue with successive heats and hammer blows. It's also possible to create special templates for making a variety of regular spirals. To bend the steel with a minimum of effort and to reduce marks left by the hammer, work the piece at a light orange color.

## MAKING A SPIRAL ON THE ANVIL

Refer to the following steps to produce a forged spiral on the end of a round rod.

**1** Hammer a heated rod that has been tapered in advance on the round horn of the anvil to create a slight curve in the tapered end.

**2** Hammer the curved steel on the face of the anvil in order to fold the end onto itself.

**3** Heat the curved end again and hammer on the face of the anvil in the direction of movement for the scroll.

**4** Adjust the curves of the spiral with gentle hammer blows while the steel is still glowing.

The end of the rod rolled into a spiral

## A Twisted Scroll

A twisted scroll is a spiral with the ends stretched out to increase its volume. The steps below illustrate how to make a spiral on the blacksmith's vise.

**1** Bend over the previously tapered end of the rod gripped in the jaws of the blacksmith's vise.

**2** Heat the rod again, hold the tapered end in the jaws of the blacksmith's vise, and begin bending the rod onto itself.

**3** Use the hammer to adjust the spiral as it continues to curve.

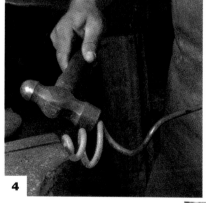

**4** The rod is pulled out once all the turns of the spiral are made. While doing this, clamp the heated spiral in the blacksmith's vise by the tapered end. Pull on the part of the rod that is still straight, helping the process with gentle hammer blows.

**5** Use a steel bar to finish evening out the distances between turns. This step can be done cold if the thickness of the rod allows.

Logical sequence for creating and stretching out a twisted scroll

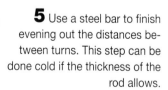

# Right-angle Bend

A right-angle bend involves creating a 90° bend in a piece of steel. The bend can be produced by hammering the heated steel directly on the anvil, as shown here, or by clamping it in the jaws of the blacksmith's vise and bending it with gentle hammer blows. Sometimes, to produce an acute angle in the corner, it's necessary to draw the metal out in advance into a tenon or start with an upset in the area where the corner is to be bent.

Bending a drawn-out piece of steel on the side of the anvil face

Sequence for creating and bending the tenon to produce a bend with an acute angle

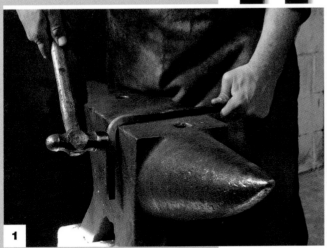

1

2

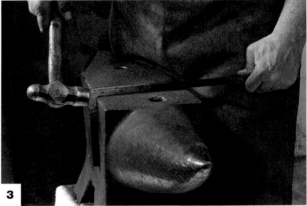

3

**1** Bending a heated piece of steel by hammering it on the side of the anvil face

**2** Upsetting the angle on the face of the anvil

**3** Adjusting the right-angle bend on the side of the anvil

# Clips

Clips are one type of joint that involve rolling a piece of steel, usually a flat strap, around other pieces of steel to hold them together. It's necessary to know the unrolled length of the clip, which corresponds to the length of its neutral fiber. This equals the sum of the rectangle's side lengths that results from combining the shapes to be joined with the length of the arcs in the clip. It's possible to make an approximate determination by measuring with a piece of string around the pieces of steel.

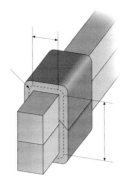 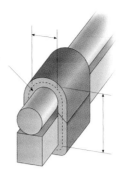

To calculate the length of the neutral fiber (the broken red line in the illustration), add together the lengths of the sides plus the lengths of the arcs to be enclosed by the strap.

Detail of the clip on a grate on a modernist mansion in Barcelona, Spain

**1** The process of installing a clip. The previously bent and heated strap is placed around the two pieces of steel to be joined.

**2** It's immediately bent around the two pieces of steel using gentle hammer blows. To avoid stretching the heated clip, don't hammer forcefully. When the steel cools, it contracts and holds the pieces together tightly.

*Basic techniques*

This section includes the techniques for cutting off material or creating holes without losing any steel. The material must be heated to the proper temperature so that it can be parted easily during forging operations. Anvil hardies and punches are necessary for the process. These are simple techniques, but they require lots of trial and error to gain experience. Of course, this is the only way to achieve high quality work.

## Trimming

Trimming is done with hammer blows on a hardy secured in the anvil. Depending on the thickness of the stock, this can be done either hot or cold. The steel must be marked at the proper distance all the way around without completing the cut entirely. The end of the piece to be cut off is then hammered on the edge of the anvil face to separate it.

Hot trimming the end of a rod to make the head of a forged nail. It was first marked out hot on the hardy at the place where the cut was to be made.

**1**

**1** The cold rod is struck with a hammer on the edge of the hardy. This process repeats on the four sides of the steel rod.

**2** The end of the piece is then hammered on the edge of the anvil face until it separates from the rest of the rod.

The steps for trimming a rod properly

**2**

## Ripping

Ripping involves parting the end of the steel using a cut of the appropriate length. The resulting division simply opens up to produce the effect of tree branching. It doesn't come off the original shape.

The piece is heated to a uniform light orange color, placed onto the hardy, and then carefully hammered on both sides so the hammer isn't damaged on the cutting edge. This operation is always done hot and as many times as necessary to produce the entire split in the steel.

**1** Start the split by hammering the strap on both sides while holding it on the hardy.

**2** Apply vertical hammer blows over the cutting edge of the hardy in order to separate the two resulting sides and continue forging the piece.

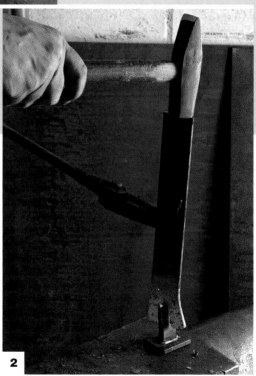

Cross in Torroella de Montgrí, Spain. Forged iron cross clearly displaying the split ends that were subsequently tapered and bent

## Splitting

Splitting involves parting the steel in the center to create openings without removing any material from the stock. The bar is heated to dark yellow, at which point the steel is softest. The rod is placed onto the hardy and hammered, turning it over to create the cut on two sides. Then it is struck vertically on the anvil to separate the resulting sides, and worked with the hammer on the conical beak to correct the shape.

**1**

**1** The glowing rod is hammered on the hardy, turning it over to cut on both sides.

**2** The bar is struck vertically on the face of the anvil to separate the two sides.

**3** The separated sides are forged on the conical beak of the anvil.

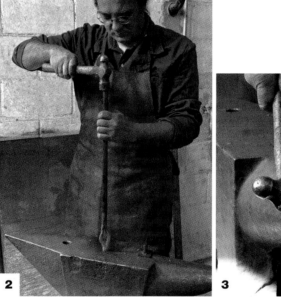

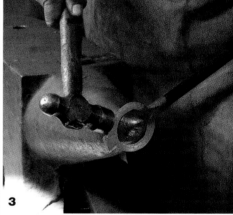

**2**

**3**

Sequence of steps in forging a split

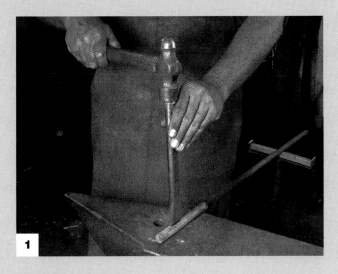

1

2

**1** The area to be punched is marked with a cold chisel. It's a good idea to support the piece with a work stand to free up your hands.

**2** The hole is punched on the round hole in the anvil face, on both sides of the rod.

**3** The pierced area is upset to preserve the thickness and limit the stretching caused by inserting the punches.

## Punching

Punching is a combination of several forging techniques. First, a split is created, then it's upset, and, finally, it's widened to create a hole of a specific diameter. The operation is carried out on the round hole in the anvil, turning the rod to start the punch on both sides. The final hole is achieved after heating the rod several times to gradually stretch it.

3

Punching sequence

Close-up of a grate showing a joint in the bars created by punching

# special cutting techniques

This section describes processes for cutting steel that are accessible to modest workshops. An oxygen cutting torch can be used to heat the metal locally in addition to cutting it. A mixture of propane or acetylene and oxygen in the torch combusts to produce heat.

Plasma cutting makes it possible to cut any metal quickly but requires a certain amount of workshop infrastructure.

## Oxygen Cutting

Oxygen cutting is designed for ferrous metals. If the temperature of the steel is raised above 1652°F (900°C), and a jet of pure oxygen is applied to it, the carbon steel combusts. The flame serves to raise the piece of steel to the ignition temperature and clean the surface of slag, oxides, and leftover paint. The jet of oxygen is then applied through the same torch to burn the metal when it reaches the ignition temperature and remove the slag formation, producing a narrow groove.

**1** The pre-heating flame is applied for a certain time to the start of the oxygen cut; the duration depends on the thickness of the material to be cut.

**2** The jet of extra oxygen is applied to produce the combustion of the steel, and the movement is begun in the direction of the cut.

**3** The same distance is maintained between the nozzle of the torch and the steel being cut, to guarantee a uniform temperature throughout the process.

Ares, *Petita història d'un cilindre*, 2005 (20 x 24 x 3 inches [50.8 x 61 x 7.6 cm]). Detail of the pieces produced by the oxygen-cutting process once the edges are ground

**1** The nozzle of the torch is placed off the piece to begin cutting. It's necessary to drill holes as starting places for the cuts for open work.

## Plasma Cutting

This cut is created with a stream of plasma produced when a gas (or mixture of gasses) passes through a narrow nozzle and is then ionized with energy supplied to it by a strangulated electric arc. In addition to the thermal action, which melts the metal with temperatures that reach 36,032°F (20,000°C), the plasma stream exerts a mechanical action as it moves at a high speed of around 3300 fps (1000 m/s), continually freeing up the melted material. Air, a mixture of nitrogen and oxygen, is most commonly used for these operations. In contrast to the oxygen-cutting process, plasma cutting makes it possible to cut any metal that conducts electricity.

**2** The ground clamp is placed on the workbench to produce the stream of plasma. The bench must allow the melted metal to flow out beneath the piece.

**3** The melted metal is liberated continually during the process through the pressure from the plasma stream; this produces a clean cut in the metal, with minimal heating.

Ares. *De l'aire*, 2006 (10⅝ x 6¾ x 4 inches [27 x 17 x 10 cm]). Produced by plasma cutting and forging

*Basic techniques*

**49**

In this process, metal is heated to a certain temperature, kept there for a time, and cooled at a specific rate. The results depend on the temperature reached and the speed of the cooling. The structure of the metal changes, which also changes its mechanical properties. What follows are heat treatments that provide no change in the composition of the metal aggregates. These are annealing, hardening, and tempering.

## Annealing

This treatment returns the properties (including ductility) the steel lost through mechanical operations such as cold hammering. The piece is heated to a specific temperature between about 392° to 1292°F (200° to 700°C), held there for a certain time, and slowly air-cooled.

## Hardening

This heat treatment increases the toughness and hardness of the metal but also its breakability. Hardening involves heating the steel evenly up to a certain temperature, between about 1382° and 1475°F (750° to 800°C), and then quickly quenching it in a bath, generally water at room temperature. The piece is plunged into the water for cooling in a very deliberate manner. The container for the liquid must be large enough to accommodate the entire piece as it is moved around. It's best to put it into the bath along its vertical axis. Its shape will determine the way to stir it around in the liquid. This treatment is very commonly used for creating tools from steel with a carbon content lower than 9.0%.

## Tempering

Tempering helps to eliminate the tensions produced by sudden expansions and contractions when the steel is hardened. It involves reheating the hardened piece to a relatively low temperature, from about 200° to 600°F (100° to 320°C), and then cooling it. In tempering, the piece loses some hardness, but it gains resilience.

Forged tools that have been hardened and tempered for working stone and marble

## Hardening a Tool for Cutting Stone

A gradine is made from a round rod of low-carbon steel (less than 0.9%) that is forged and hardened by the blacksmith to be used for working stone. The process of heat-treating tools requires lots of observation and practice.

**1** The steel rod is heated and pounded out on the face of the anvil. This involves broadening and tapering the end of the rod that subsequently will be hardened.

**2** Once the end is forged, the electric bench grinder is used to create a cutting edge, using a fine-grit wheel.

**3** A hacksaw is used to create the teeth of the gradine. The number and size of the teeth will depend on how coarse you want the tool to be. The relative coarseness or fineness would be based on the hardness of the material to be cut and whether you were roughing it out or coming close to final dimensions and surface appearance (coarse and fine teeth, respectively).

**4** Heat the part of the piece to be hardened. Since the steel has to heat up slowly and uniformly, keep turning it over in the forge. When the piece reaches cherry red, it's at the hardening temperature, between 1310° and 1562°F (710° and 850°C). Plunge the rod into the quench (water) vertically and in a straight line. Note how the hardening colors climb up the steel. (Please refer back to illustration on page 20.)

# BASIC WELDING TECHNIQUES

Gaining familiarity with welding techniques is possible only through intensive practice. People who work with welding equipment must protect themselves against ultraviolet ray emission, red-hot sparks, and burns. In this section you will learn the two most common welding techniques used in small workshops.

## welding with **coated rod**

Welding with a coated rod is one of the most accessible techniques because the necessary equipment is easy to find. In this process, the metal is fused through heat generated by an electric arc, also referred to as a voltaic arc, set up between the end of the coated electrode and the metal base. This process requires great skill and practice to control all the parameters.

### The Coated Rod

The electrode is responsible for setting up the voltaic arc, protecting the fusion bath, and contributing the material for the joint. It's made from a metal rod covered with a material consisting of various chemical substances. The most common type is made from **rutile** (a form of titanium dioxide). For welding steel, a metal rod made from different ferrous materials is used for joining the edges of pieces by fusion.

The coating stabilizes the voltaic arc and creates gases that protect the fusion bath. It forms a slag that covers the bead of weld to prevent sudden cooling, which could cause cracks, and it simultaneously keeps this red-hot area from contacting the oxygen and nitrogen in the air. This will cause the bead to oxidize and will create pores inside it, thereby weakening it.

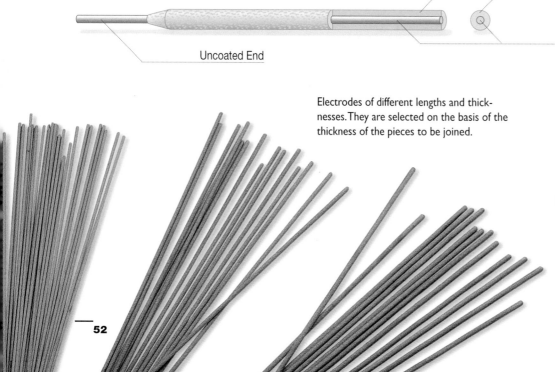

Cross-section of a coated rod

Coating

Metal Core

Uncoated End

Electrodes of different lengths and thicknesses. They are selected on the basis of the thickness of the pieces to be joined.

Electrodes have four digits imprinted on them to indicate their properties. In this case, the label shows that this is an electrode with a rutile coating and a resistance to traction of around 4085 lbs./sq. in. (43 kg/mm2), appropriate for welding in any position.

OMNIA 46 / 6013

# Basic Aspects of Welding Technique

On this page we present some aspects of basic welding techniques.

### ELECTRODE PLACEMENT
The uncoated part of the electrode is placed in the clamp of the electrode holder. Because there is still tension (voltage) in the clamp even when you are not welding, wear protective gloves to avoid the risk of an electric shock.

### STARTING THE WELD
To begin welding, place the end of the electrode held in the clamp into contact with the pieces of steel to be welded, which are held by the ground clamp. This is called priming. The voltaic arc is established, the fusion bath is created, and this forms the welding bead that joins the pieces. A side-to-side motion is applied to the electrode while welding.

### SAFETY
Throughout the welding process, it's necessary to wear a leather apron and gloves, for protection against sparks, and a mask with a non-actinic glass for protection against ultraviolet rays produced by the fusion bath.

Placing the electrode into the clamp. Protective gloves are used to guard against possible electric discharge.

To begin welding, the electrode is tapped lightly at the point where the weld is to begin and is immediately pulled back slightly to establish the electric arc.

Proper eye protection, an apron, and gloves will ensure safety during welding.

A    B    C    D

Diagram showing the movements of the electrode: A) circular; B) semicircular; C) zigzag; and D) interlaced

*Basic techniques*

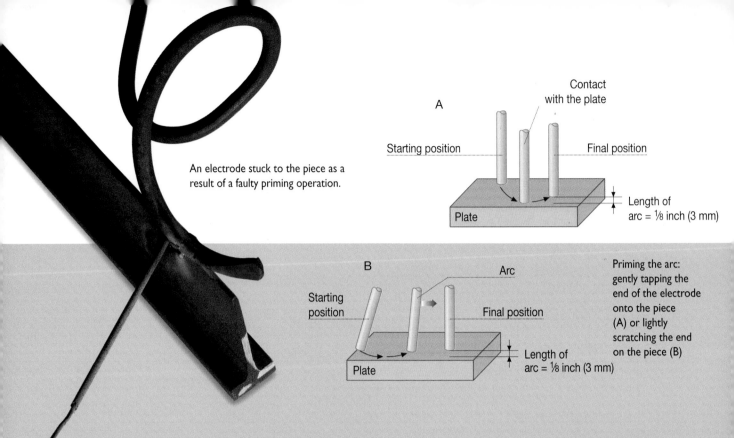

An electrode stuck to the piece as a result of a faulty priming operation.

A

Starting position

Contact with the plate

Final position

Length of arc = ⅛ inch (3 mm)

Plate

B

Arc

Starting position

Final position

Length of arc = ⅛ inch (3 mm)

Plate

Priming the arc: gently tapping the end of the electrode onto the piece (A) or lightly scratching the end on the piece (B)

## Priming the Arc

Priming involves lightly tapping the tip of the electrode onto the piece to be welded (connected to the ground clamp) and immediately pulling it back a distance equal to the diameter of the electrode. This establishes the voltaic arc and begins the weld. No matter what technique is used to prime, it's important to immediately lift the electrode to the proper height to set up the arc. Otherwise, the electrode sticks to the piece and quickly gets red hot from the electric current passing through it. If this happens, quickly release it from the electrode clamp or detach it from the piece. Because of the intense light, these steps must be done without removing the face shield from the eyes.

After the voltaic arc is established, proceed with the proper speed, intensity, electrode angle, and arc length. Be sure not to go too slowly and waste welding rod by creating too coarse a bead, or too fast, which may prevent an even, uniform bead. A sense for the proper speed will develop through practice. The characteristic sputtering of the welding process will affirm that everything is correct.

Illustration of the welding process with coated rod once the arc is primed

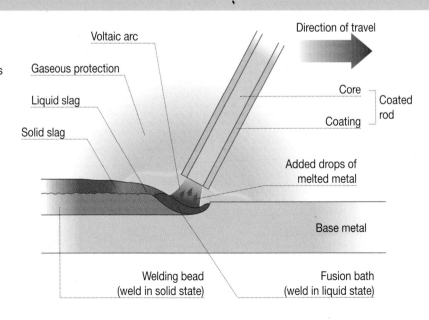

Direction of travel

Voltaic arc

Gaseous protection

Liquid slag

Solid slag

Core

Coated rod

Coating

Added drops of melted metal

Base metal

Welding bead (weld in solid state)

Fusion bath (weld in liquid state)

# Welding Parameters

Several parameters dictate the process of welding with coated rod.

The **diameter** of the electrode is chosen with respect to the thickness of the material, the joint, and the position of the weld. Generally, thin electrodes should be used on thin pieces and on the initial spots for joints.

The **intensity** of the current in the welding process affects the degree of penetration of the weld into the base metal. The greater the intensity, the greater the resulting penetration. When welding at an angle, the intensity must be far greater than in other positions in order to ensure that the fusion bath penetrates adequately.

The **length of the voltaic** arc influences the quality of the weld. In general, it should be the same as the diameter of the electrode.

The **speed of travel** during the welding process must allow the arc to go slightly ahead of the fusion bath. This will prevent overheating and will produce narrow beads of weld that cool quickly.

The **angle** is defined in two ways: by the longitudinal inclination formed by the electrode and the bead of weld, and by lateral inclination formed by the electrode and the pieces to be soldered together. If the angle isn't correct, slag may get inside the bead.

Crystallized slag typical of welding with coated rod

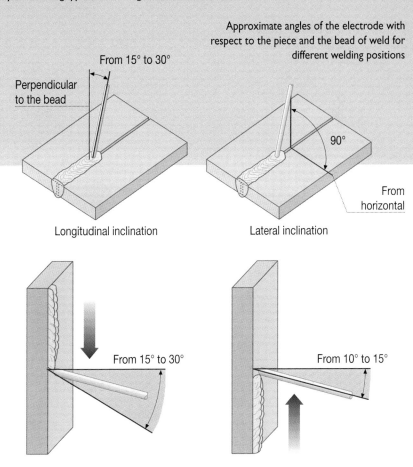

Approximate angles of the electrode with respect to the piece and the bead of weld for different welding positions

*Basic techniques*

# oxy-gas welding

The energy for the fusion in the oxy-gas welding process comes from heat produced by a flame from the combustion of a gas and oxygen. The most commonly used gases are oxygen and acetylene. This combination generates a temperature of almost 5800°F (3200°C). The flame heats the pieces to be joined until the contact areas melt, producing a bead of weld.

Oxy-gas welding can be done with or without adding metal. When metal is added, it's applied in the form of metal rods, generally of the same type as the base metal. It's well suited for joining thin pieces and for strong welds in copper or brass.

## OBSERVATIONS ON SETTING UP THE EQUIPMENT

The manometers for different gases shouldn't be switched between different tanks, and all safety instructions provided by the gas tank distributors should be faithfully followed.

The torch must have a built-in check valve to keep the flame from backing up.

The manometers must be regulated with respect to the diameter of the nozzle. In general, the oxygen is adjusted to a working pressure around 4.4 to 6.6 pounds per square inch (2 to 3 kg/cm2); the pressure for acetylene falls between about 1¾ and 3 ounces per square inch (50 and 100 g/cm2).

Goggles and face shield are necessary for reducing the effect of the bright light during the welding operation

Welding torch and interchangeable nozzles; different diameter nozzels are used for different thicknesses of the pieces to be welded. Note the check valve for the flame located between the body of the torch and the hoses.

Pressure manometers on the opening and closing valves of the oxygen and acetylene tanks

## THE FLAME

There are two distinct parts of the flame. One is the bright, dazzling white cone, where the combustion of the acetylene and oxygen takes place; the other is the plume that surrounds the cone and protects the fusion bath. There is a third area that is not perceptible to the naked eye known as the work area; it is located immediately beyond the cone, and it is the area of highest temperature.

## LIGHTING THE TORCH

Open the gas valves on the tank of acetylene. Then, open the valve controlling the gas. The acetylene is ignited with a lighter or a match. The oxygen valve is opened slowly to produce a neutral flame of an equal amount of acetylene and oxygen. Remember to use the goggles for protection against the intense light. To turn off the torch, close the acetylene valve first, and then the oxygen valve.

## OPERATING TECHNIQUE

The cone of the flame is brought to within 3/32 to 1/8 inch (2 to 3 mm) of the base piece to cause the fusion of the two edges. A subtle turning of the cone at the instant the edges flow causes them to fuse. The resulting drop is pushed with the pressure from the cone at a 45° angle with respect to the welding bead to weld without adding metal.

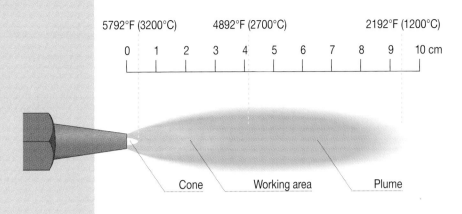

The parts of the flame and the relationship among the temperatures and the distance from the cone

The relationship of the angle between the metal being welded and the cone during the oxy-gas welding process: without adding metal (A) and using a rod to supply metal (B)

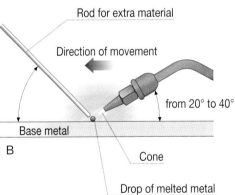

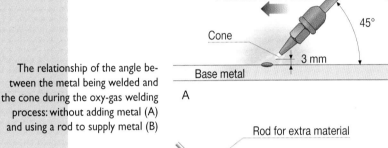

Rods for added material used in oxy-gas welding with carbon steel.

# Step
# by step

The following step-by-step sequences will show how to make forged items using the techniques explained in previous chapters. These are practical exercises for understanding and applying various techniques.

# Cold forging
# a **trivet**

Making a simple but practical trivet serves as an introduction to the cold forging techniques. A sheet of ⁹⁄₃₂ inch (2 mm) thick steel will be cut into strips. These can be twisted without having to be heated, arranged in a grid pattern, and held together with self-tapping screws.

**1** Start with a sketch at the outset of the exercise.

**2** Use a scratch awl and a metal rule to mark strips about ⁹⁄₁₆ inch (1.5 cm) wide on a reused sheet of steel.

**3** Use a shear to cut out the strips along the marked lines. Be sure to wear leather gloves.

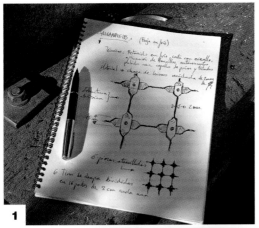

**4** Straighten the strips by hammering them on the anvil.

**5** File the strips to remove the sharp edges.

**6** To identify where the twists will be made, mark the strips into ¾-inch (2 cm) segments with a square and a scratch awl.

4

5

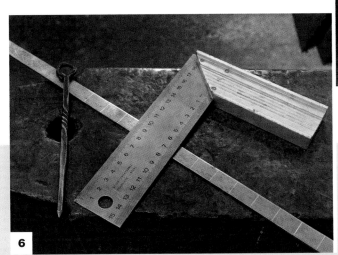

6

**7** Divide the strip into segments about a foot (30 cm) long, and use the bench grinder to grind the ends round.

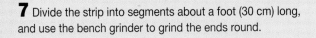

7

8

**8** Use a bending tool to start the twist in each section of the strip held in the blacksmith's vise. The divisions previously scribed indicate the intervals between twists.

**9** The twists are made in the same direction until the entire strip is done.

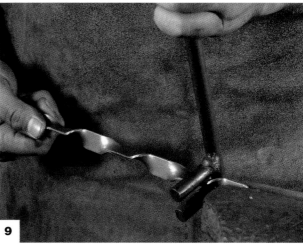

9

**10** The strips are the same length because of the marks made prior to cutting and twisting.

**11** A round file is used to shape any imperfections.

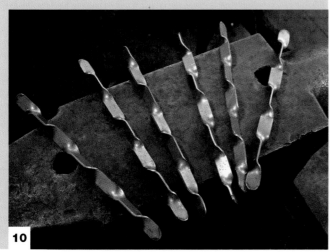

10

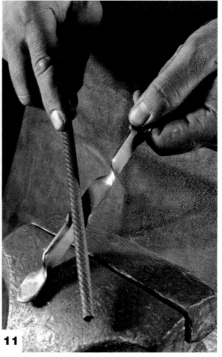

11

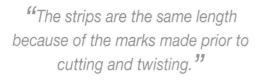

*"The strips are the same length because of the marks made prior to cutting and twisting."*

**12** On the square beak of the anvil, use a center punch to mark every strip for the holes where they will all be joined together.

**13** Drill these holes with an electric drill, using a bit slightly smaller than the self-tapping screw that will be used to connect the strips.

12

13

14

**14** Remove the burrs produced by drilling with a fine file.

**15** Follow the pattern of one turn ahead and a half-turn back to cut the threads properly in the strip and install the screws.

**16** Screw the strips together, keeping the screw slots parallel to one another to create a harmonious effect.

15

16

**17** Use an angle grinder to cut away the remainder of the screw projecting through the sheet metal.

**18** Use a wire brush chucked up in an electric drill to even out the surface of the trivet.

17

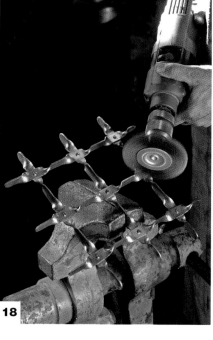
18

**19** Apply a transparent aerosol varnish to protect the metal from rust. Once it's dry, apply a coat of wax to cut down on the glare from the metal.

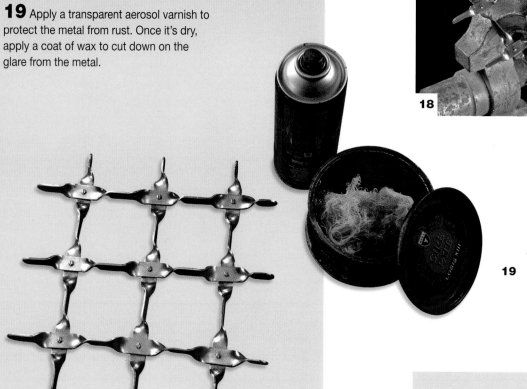
19

*The finished trivet*

# door
# pull

Fabricating a door pull will demonstrate the basic techniques of hot twisting and rolling. The pull will consist of a twisted central part and two scrolls at the ends made from a rod about ⅜ inch (10 mm) in diameter and 3¼ feet (100 cm) long. Screws will also be made to attach it to the door.

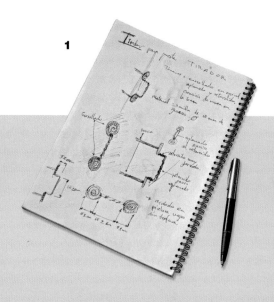

**1**

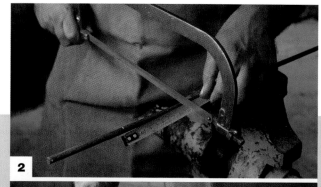

**1** Make a couple of sketches of the door pull you want to produce, and apply the measurements and techniques chosen in planning the project.

**2** Divide the steel rod into seven equal parts, using a hacksaw and making light cuts.

**3** Place the heated rod into the blacksmith's vise and bend the two ends to 90° angle with a hammer.

**4** Flatten the center of the rod by hammering it on the face of the anvil.

**5** Turn the rod as it flattens to shape it in cross-section.

**6** Start the bend for the spiral by supporting the bent part of the rod in the blacksmith's vise and striking it with the hammer.

**7** Strike the heated rod with the hammer to roll up the spiral, working continually at a bright red heat.

**8** Occasionally, hammer the spiral gently to even it out.

**9** The first spiral is done when you get to the flattened part of the door pull.

**10** Clamp the other end of the rod in the blacksmith's vise to make the second spiral.

**11** Make the second spiral using the same process as the first one.

*"The spiral is rolled up by striking the heated rod with the hammer. It works best to continually work the spiral at a bright red heat."*

10

11

12

**12** Use water to cool the material where it's held.

**13** The second spiral is completed when you reach the flat part of the door pull.

13

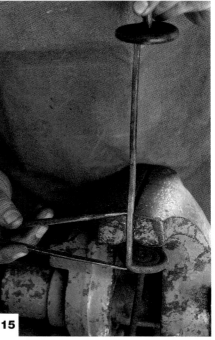

**14** The middle of the rod is bent perpendicular to the spirals to make the handle of the door pull.

**15** The compass is used to quickly mark the place where the handle must be bent.

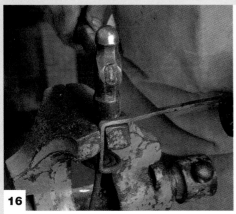

**16** With a hammer, bend a part of the handle at red heat on the blacksmith's vise.

**17** The other end of the handle is bent using the same technique so that the spirals orient to the same direction.

**18** At this stage of the process, the rod is modified as shown in the photo.

**19** Place the heated door pull into the blacksmith's vise, and clamp it by a spiral. Use flat-jaw tongs to move the spirals to the outside of the door pull.

**20** Do this to each end of the door pull.

**21** Using the tongs, gently twist the handle.

**22** Use a bending tool to accentuate the twist on the sides of the spirals.

**23** Cut several threads on the ends of the spirals to attach the pull to the door.

*A synthetic exterior enamel will give the door pull the perfect finish.*

# fireplace
# tongs

Making fireplace tongs will demonstrate the basic forging techniques of drawing out a tenon, bending, hammering out, and riveting. The tongs will be made from two strips of steel, each ⅛ inch thick, ¾ inch wide, and 2¾ inches long (3 x 20 x 70 mm), and will have loop ends. The upper loop is used for holding and operating the jaws while the lower part comes in contact with the heat and houses the central hinge.

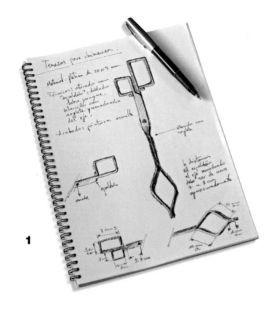

**1** The tongs are designed on a piece of paper.

**2** Make the loop ends first. Mark the straps where the tenon will start.

**3** Heat the steel and strike it on the edge of the anvil to mark out the start of the piece to be drawn out.

**4** On the anvil, vigorously hammer the strap at bright red heat to draw it out from the point indicated.

**5** Draw out the whole length to make the loop ends of the tongs.

**6** While drawing out the steel, it's a good idea to turn it over to keep the surfaces even.

**7** Form the loop for one side of the tongs in the tang and the drawn-out tenon.

**8** Put a finishing curl into the end of the loop. First, fold over the tip of the drawn-out section of strap on the edge of the anvil face.

8

9

**9** Roll the strap back onto itself by lightly hammering on the previously bent tip.

**10** On the flat surface of the anvil, strike the top of the spiral so that it will have a square outline.

**11** Continue shaping the square inside the spiral by hammering it on the corner of the anvil face.

10

*"While drawing out the steel, it's a good idea to turn it over to keep the surfaces even."*

11

**12** Start the loop for the tongs on the square beak of the anvil. Use a compass to mark the spot where the loop will be bent.

**13** Turn over the loop for the tongs to produce a 90° angle.

**14** Complete the loop by closing up the square. Proceed in the same way for the other arm of the tongs, following the design.

**15** The completed loops.

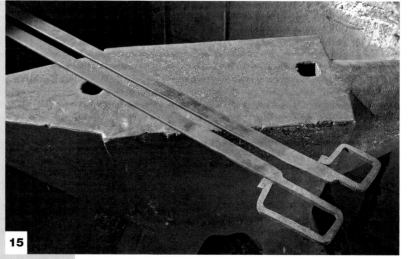

**16** On the edge of the anvil, fashion the arms of the tongs from the jaws by marking the ends of each arm.

**17** The tips of the jaws are upset to produce a rounded shape.

**18** To produce a triangular curve in the arm, it's heated and bent with the help of a fork inserted into the square anvil hold.

**19** Using the first arm as a guide, bend the second one.

*"The head of the rivet is finished off in a heading tool."*

**20**

**21**

**20** Make the pivot for the tongs in the form of a rivet. Hold a piece of ¼-inch (6 mm) rod in the jaws of the vise. Heat the rod with a torch while it is upset by hammering.

**21** Finish off the head of the rivet in a heading tool.

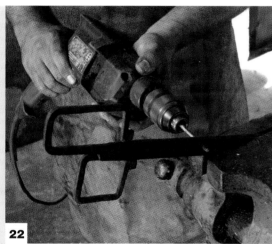

**22**

**24**

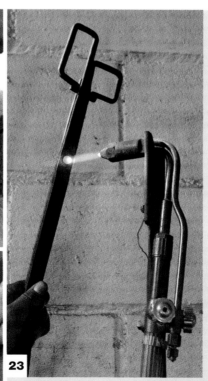

**23**

**22** Use an electric drill with a bit smaller than half the width of the arm to drill the hole for the pivot. The arms of the tongs will pivot on this point.

**23** Put the pin into the hole, cut it to the appropriate length, and heat it with a torch.

**24** Immediately upon heating, upset the pivot to shape the head of the pin. Perform the operation on a base plate installed in the square hole of the anvil.

*Step by step*

**25** In finishing the tongs, the arms are bent at 90° to the pivot point for proper functioning. They are heated at the point for the twist, using a torch to localize the heat more effectively.

**26** The tongs are twisted using a bending tool while they are clamped in the blacksmith's vise.

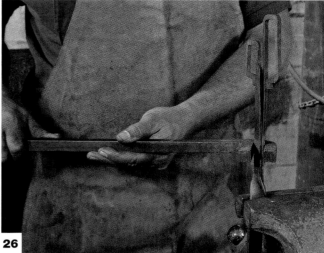

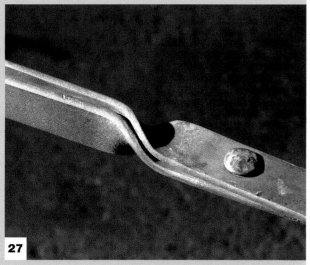

**27** Detail of the twisted area

*Fireplace tongs painted with*
*flat black enamel*

# grate with
# **volutes**

The following example, a grate with two symmetrical sides, is taken from a forged railing on an interior patio of a building in Spain, a restoration project by Valeria Cortes. Templates are constructed cold for each volute, on which the steel straps will be forged. The two volutes are then welded together, framed inside straps of steel, and connected to it with clamps to produce the grate. All templates are made in the same manner.

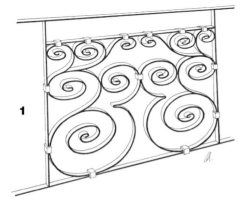

**1** Make a drawing of the volutes in the grill to produce a general idea of the final result.

**2** On a sheet of plywood, draw the volutes to size in the desired shape.

**3** To make the grate, construct a metal template in the shape of the volutes. Using a bending tool and bending hook, curve a thin strap of steel.

**4** At the same time, check the curves produced in the steel strap against the drawing on the piece of plywood.

1

2

3

4

**5** and **6** Weld the resulting strips to a steel plate that has a piece of steel welded to the bottom that will fit into the square hole in the anvil. Weld the strap steel to the sheet in two phases to allow forging every curve of the volute.

**7** Using a section of rope placed on the line drawn on the wood, determine the approximate length of the steel strapping needed for making the volute.

**8** Stretch the rope along the steel strapping, and use a piece of chalk to mark off the distance to cut. Because two volutes will be made on the same template at the same time, perform this step (and those below) on two pieces of strapping at the same time.

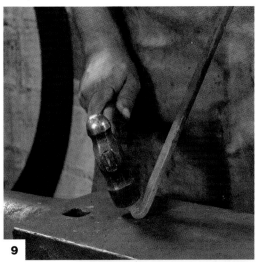

**9** To make the first volute, heat the tip of the selected steel strapping and bend it slightly on the face of the anvil.

**10** Heat the strapping again and hook it into the start of the template; forge the first curve by exerting pressure on the template.

**11** As the curves of the volutes are forged, the templates are welded to the steel plate.

**12** Make sure that the material doesn't heat up to the melting point by taking it out of the fire at the proper temperature, as demonstrated by the color of the metal in the picture.

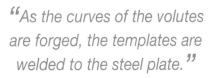

*"As the curves of the volutes are forged, the templates are welded to the steel plate."*

**13** Heat the strapping in the forge and work it on the anvil, following the template for each curve of the volute.

**14** Use a flat piece of steel as a lever to remove the forged strapping from the template.

**15** Make every curve of the volute in duplicate, since the grate will have two symmetrical parts.

**16** After finishing every volute, use the proper tongs to hold the red-hot steel, and hammer it to form to the template.

**17** Complete the last curve of the volute by pressing the strapping against the template with the tongs.

15

**18**

**19**

**18** Place the spiral onto the plywood drawing. Use a piece of chalk to mark the point where the extra strapping will be cut off.

**19** Use a cutting wheel to cut off the spiral at the chalk mark.

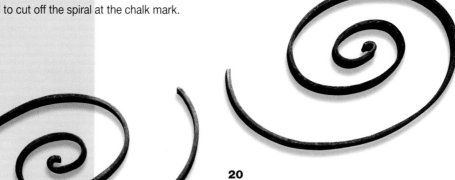

**20**

**20** Finish the volutes made on the same template, after trimming the ends to length.

**21** Using a square, attach steel rods to a sheet of steel to temporarily arrange the volutes.

**21**

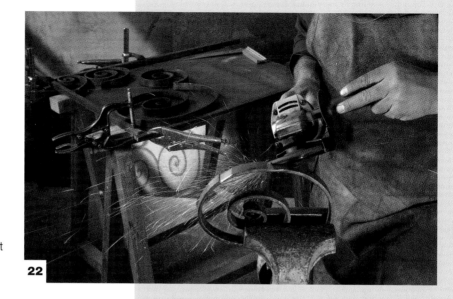

*"Make sure that the material does not heat up to the melting point."*

**22** Make the slots where the volutes fit together with an angle grinder.

**23** Close-up of how the volutes fit together. The shiny area that was ground is the place where the volutes will be welded together. Note the slight bevel on the edge of the strapping to make room for the weld.

**24** Continue grinding every volute individually, and fit them together on the temporary plate.

**25** The finished volutes and frame after being fit together on the steel plate according to the initial drawing.

**26** Hold the volutes together by welding with coated rod. Take particular care in priming the arc on the volutes to avoid any movement in their alignment.

**27** The bead of weld at the joint between two volutes. Note the crystallized slag that is typical of welding with coated rod.

**28** Go over the welds with an angle grinder to even out the surfaces.

26

27

28

29

**29** The grate after the welds at the joints between volutes have been ground.

**30** The clamps to hold the volutes to the frame of the grate are now made. Once you determine the length of the neutral fiber, make a sample and try it out.

**31** Heat the strapping with a torch on a die block made to dimensions for fabricating numerous clamps of the same size.

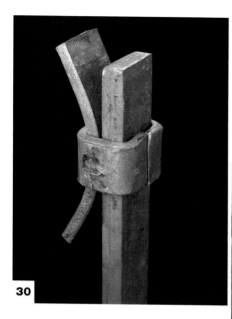

30

31

32

*"When it cools, the clamp shrinks, thereby increasing its grip and strength."*

**32** and **33** To create the U shape, hammer the heated clamp into the die block with a bar made for the purpose.

33

*Step by step*

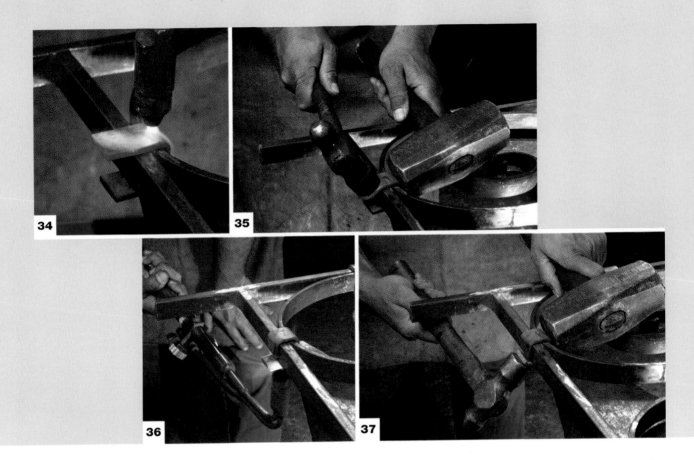

**34** Place the bent clamp at the point on the frame where it touches a curve of the volute. Heat it with the torch. The frame that will hold the volutes by means of the clamps has been constructed.

**35** Start bending and closing the heated part of the clamp by hammering it; a sledge hammer held behind it will keep the volute from separating.

**36** and **37** Heat the rest of the clamp and continue working as in the previous step.

**38** The clamp shrinks as it cools, increasing its grip and strength.

*Grill of volutes installed in a building in Spain. It was finished with a coat of reddish antirust paint to simulate oxidized iron.*

## wall
# candelabrum

We will show how to make a hanging candelabrum in this step-by-step exercise. It consists of three parts: the bracket from which the candelabrum hangs, the candelabrum itself, and a connector that holds it to the bracket. We'll use the techniques of splitting, perforating, bending, flattening, tapering, and cutting while combining traditional techniques with modern processes. For example, we'll use the flame from a torch to apply heat to a specific spot, and we'll use an angle-grinder to cut a groove.

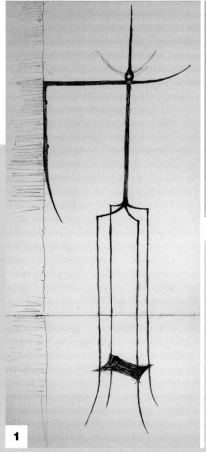

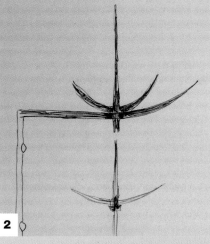

**1** and **2** Plan the candelabrum project with the aid of a couple of drawings. The sketches will serve as a guide for the work.

**3** Start the split by marking the center of the heated rod with a cold chisel and a hammer on the face of the anvil.

**4**

**5**

**4** When the rod is at yellow-red heat, hammer it on a hardy in the anvil, and split it in the middle.

**6**

**7**

**5** Next, strike the tip of the heated bar vertically on the anvil to open the two sides of the split.

**6** Place the opening on the round anvil beak, and hammer the tip of the rod to produce a rounded shape.

**7** Use gentle hammer blows to refine the shape on the round beak.

*Step by step*

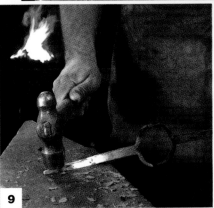

*"Gentle hammer blows are used to refine the shape."*

**8** Heat the end of the split, rod and taper it by hammering forcefully on the face of the anvil.

**9** and **10** Keep turning the rod while hammering to create a uniform point on the tapered end.

**11** Measure the precise spot on the rod to bend to a 90° angle. When the rod reaches a red heat, use a bending tool on the anvil to create the bracket shape.

**12** After heating, slightly taper and curve the opposite end.

**13** Flatten out the areas for the screws that will attach the bracket to the wall. Heat the selected area, and hammer forcefully on the round beak.

**14** Once the flats are in place, it's necessary to straighten the rod by heating it and hammering it on the face of the anvil.

**15** Detail of the flattened areas where the bracket will be attached to the wall

**16** A view of the completed bracket

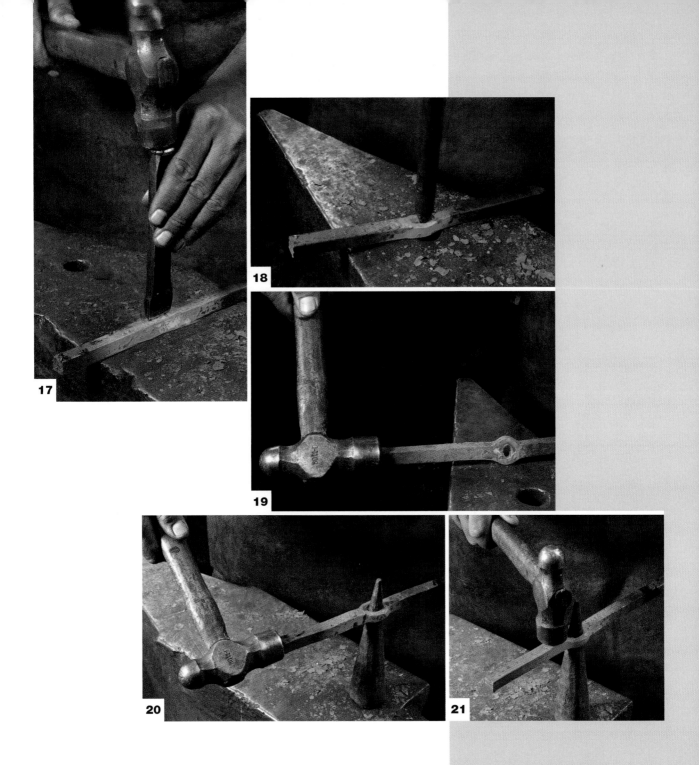

**17** To make the main part of the candelabrum, punch a hole in the square rod when it has been heated to yellow-red. Mark the area first.

**18** Place the rod over the round hole in the anvil face, and make a hole by striking the spot with a punch.

**19** As the hole is punched, it's necessary to upset the area to counteract the stretching produced by the punching operation.

**20** and **21** To produce a uniform hole, adjust it on an anvil tool so that you can hammer in all directions.

**22** Draw out the end of the rod near the hole to create a tapered point on the candelabrum.

**23** Use a hardy with a rounded end to mark the place on the rod where it will be hammered out.

**24** To hammer out the rod, strike it on a flat stake held in the anvil.

22

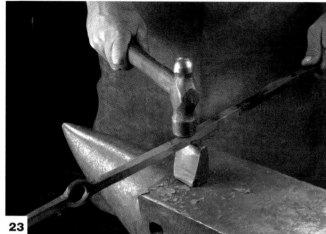

23

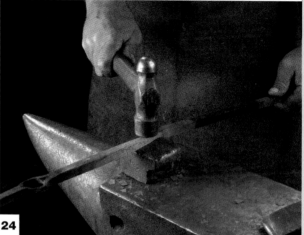

24

*"As the hole is punched, it is necessary to upset the area."*

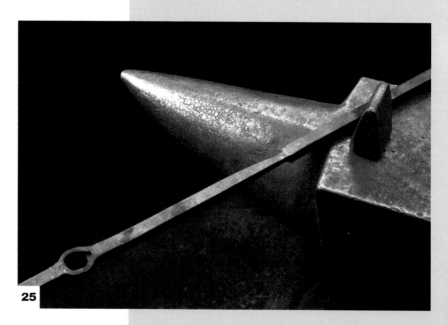

**25** Detail of the inner part before hammering out. Use a cutting wheel to make some grooves in the part of the rod that is not hammered out.

25

*Step by step*

95

**27**

**28**

**26**

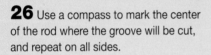

**26** Use a compass to mark the center of the rod where the groove will be cut, and repeat on all sides.

**27** Go over the lines marked with the compass with an angle grinder and a thin cutting wheel to produce a groove sufficiently straight and deep to keep the disk from running off course.

**28** Produce the cut with several passes of the grinder on the sides of the rod.

**29** Heat the resulting ends of the groove, and then separate and bend to a 90° angle to the main axis.

**29**

**30**

**31**

**32**

**30** Once the sides are separated, go over them with a file to remove the rough edges produced by the grinder.

**31** Heat and taper the ends on the face of the anvil.

**32** Measure from the center and heat with a torch. Next, bend at the heated area using flat-jawed tongs.

*"Go over the lines marked with the compass to produce a sufficiently straight groove."*

**33** The finished central part of the candelabrum

**33**

**34**

**35**

**36**

**34** To begin the connector that will hold the candelabrum so it hangs from the bracket, first taper the end of an appropriately sized rod.

**35** Clamp the rod in the jaws of a blacksmith's vise, and cut off the excess from the opposite end with a cutting wheel.

**36** Hold the rod with tongs, to avoid burning your hands, and taper the opposite end.

**37**

**38**

**37** and **38** Heat the ends, and use tongs and a hammer to slightly curve them on the round anvil beak.

*"Holding the rod with tongs to avoid burning the hands, taper the opposite end."*

**39** Use a plasma cutter to cut out a piece of sheet steel. To produce a straight cut, use a piece of angle iron as a guide for resting the plasma torch.

**40** Heat the corners of the sheet steel, and curve them by striking them on the round beak of the anvil.

**41** Use an electric drill to make holes in the curved ends, holding the sheet in the jaws of the blacksmith's vise.

**42** Detail of the steel plate that will hold the candle

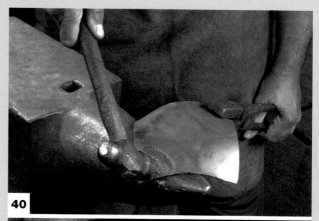

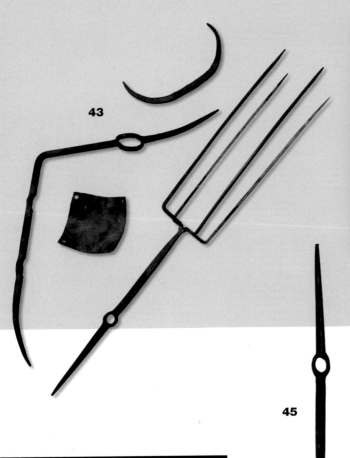

**43**

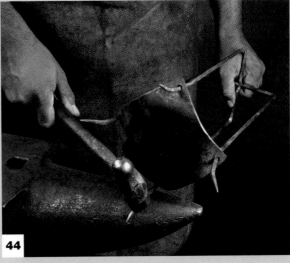

**44**

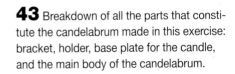

**45**

**46**

**43** Breakdown of all the parts that constitute the candelabrum made in this exercise: bracket, holder, base plate for the candle, and the main body of the candelabrum.

**44** The main body sides are fit into the holes in the base plate and bent cold by gently hammering on the round anvil beak.

**45** The assembled main part of the candelabrum.

**46** Detail of the junction involving the holder, the main body, and the bracket

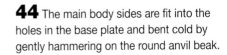

*The candelabrum installed on a wall. It was finished with a graphite patina.*

# Step by Step

# door
# knocker

This step-by-step exercise will produce a reptile-shaped door knocker from a single section of round steel rod. Nails and a base plate are forged for attaching the knocker to the door. The pieces necessary to make the knocker work are forged as well. Basic techniques will combine with modern procedures such as oxy-gas cutting.

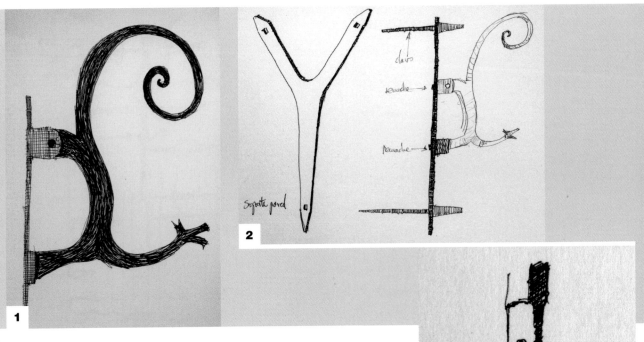

**1** Sketch the main body of the knocker, the lizard, which will be hammered out from a single piece of steel.

**2** Sketch the base plate for the knocker and how it attaches to the door.

**3** Detail of how to attach the knocker to the base and make it work

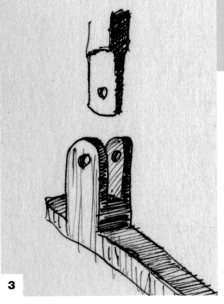

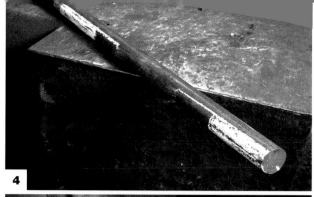

**4** Use white chalk to mark the areas of the rod where the oxygen cutting will be done. The parts with the chalk will be cut off entirely.

**5** Use the oxygen torch to cut off the marked areas; use appropriate goggles as protection against the intense light.

**6** The piece after cutting, along with the discarded pieces, previously colored white. The cuts in the rod mark out the various parts of the lizard: legs, tail, neck, and head.

**7** Spread the cuts in the end by heating the rod and striking it along the cut line on a tall hardy.

Step by step

**8** and **9** Hammer and taper the part that will become the lizard's tail. In so doing, the long part previously spread is heated and hammered forcefully on the face of the anvil. Use appropriate tongs to hold the piece securely.

**10** Hammer out the opposite end for the lizard's neck. Before that, the steel is spread in the area of the torch cut, as in the previous case.

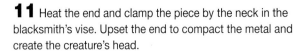

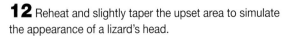

**11** Heat the end and clamp the piece by the neck in the blacksmith's vise. Upset the end to compact the metal and create the creature's head.

**12** Reheat and slightly taper the upset area to simulate the appearance of a lizard's head.

**13**

**14**

**13** and **14** Heat the part that corresponds to the front legs. Flatten it and upset the metal simultaneously to produce a rectangular shape.

**15** Hammer out the corresponding part of the hind legs, which will activate the door knocker on the base attached to the door.

**15**

*"You will have to use appropriate tongs to hold the piece securely."*

**16**

**16** The appearance of the lizard made from just one piece.

**17**

**18**

*"The tail is curled on the face of the anvil by heating it and gently hammering it."*

**19**

**17** Hold the piece by the neck in the blacksmith's vise. Make a cut in the head with a hacksaw.

**18** Heat the cut area and separate the jaws of the mouth by hammering on a hardy.

**19** Curl the tail on the face of the anvil by heating it and gently hammering it as many times as necessary to produce the desired spirals.

**20** To finish off the shape of the lizard, round the back by heating it and hammering it on the rounded beak of the anvil. The length of the hind leg has also been adjusted.

**20**

**21** To make the nails and the base for attaching the knocker to the door, hammer the end of a rod until it is the same size in cross section as the hole in the heading tool.

**22** After the nail is cut off the rest of the rod, heat and upset the part that will become the head. Repeat this for all the nails required to hold the knocker to the door.

**23** To hold the lizard in place, split a piece of previously tapered steel strapping along a cut made with an electric jigsaw. Drill a small hole at the end of the cut to make it easier to spread the sections apart.

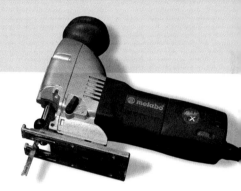

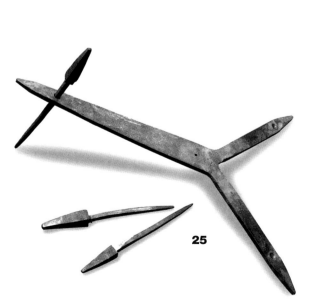

**23**

**24** Separate the two parts along the cut by heating and hammering on the rounded beak of the anvil.

**25** The finished base plate and the fastening nails. Note that the spread ends of the base have been tapered. An electric drill was also used to make holes in the ends.

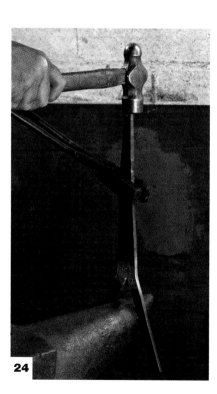

**25**

**26** The knocker will strike this anvil. It is the end of a square rod, upset, slightly tapered, and then taken down to a smaller diameter with a grinder.

**27** This part will be used to work the knocker. It consists of the tapered end of a square rod with two hacksaw cuts and a hole made with an electric drill. The material between the two cuts and the hole is removed to accommodate the back part of the lizard. Another hole has also been made in one side to receive a pin with an upset in one end to serve as a pivot for the knocker.

26

27

28

29

**28** Detail demonstrating the two previous features attached to the base plate on the door. The base plate has countersunk holes for inserting the ground-down areas; they are riveted after being heated and shaped.

**29** Detail of how the knocker works

*The door knocker installed. For protection it has been given a coat of varnish consisting of wax and colophony rosin that evens out the colors and highlights the hand-forged texture.*

# coat
# stand

This exercise will produce a coat stand that is shaped like a plant. First, make a model out of sheet metal stock to check its functionality. Using an oxy-propane torch for the forging will demonstrate another way to heat the steel. Plasma cutting will be used to taper the ends of the sheet stock. Finally, the forged sheets will be welded together using coated rod.

**1** and **2** Make scale drawings of the coat stand and the pieces that go into it.

**3** From the measurements figured in the drawing, create a full-scale model to make it easier to visualize the coat stand and how it works.

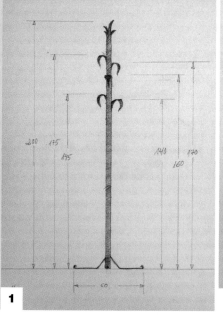

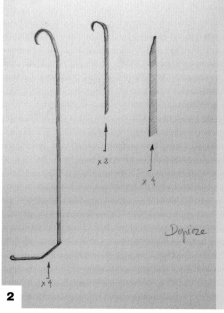

**4** Draw the outlines of each part of the coat stand in actual size on a flat surface, such as a sheet of steel. This will serve as a template for checking the work as you go along.

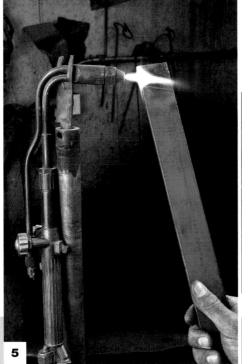

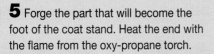

**5** Forge the part that will become the foot of the coat stand. Heat the end with the flame from the oxy-propane torch.

**6** Bend the heated end on the rounded beak of the anvil.

**7** Finish bending the end by hammering it on the face of the anvil.

**8** The finished foot of the coat stand after several heats.

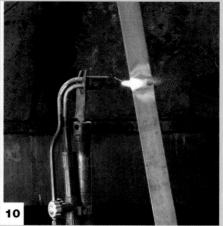

**9** Place the forged strap onto the sheet-steel drawing, and use a piece of chalk to mark the place where it is to be bent.

**10** Heat the area previously marked.

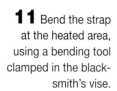

**11** Bend the strap at the heated area, using a bending tool clamped in the black-smith's vise.

**12** The rest of the bends are done in the same way: mark the pieces on the draw-ing, heat them, and bend them on the blacksmith's vise.

**13** During the construction process it's a good idea to keep checking the shape of the strap against the sheet-steel drawing.

*"The strap can rest on a support stand while you heat it."*

14

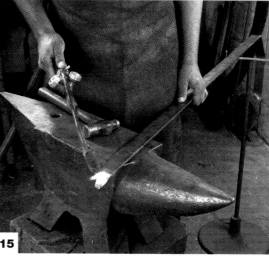

15

16

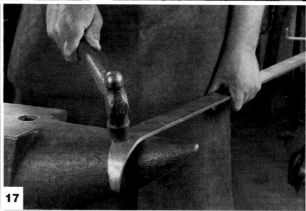

17

18

**14** Use the plasma cutter to remove part of the end of the straps to create a fairly tapered point.

**15** Place the trimmed end onto the face of the anvil, and heat it with the torch flame. The strap can rest on a support stand while you heat it. Work carefully to avoid heating up the anvil.

**16** Hammer the cut and heated end to produce a tapered, forged finish.

**17** Heat it again, and curve the end of the strap on the rounded beak of the anvil.

**18** Once the strap has cooled, give it a slight curve by levering it in a bending tool held in the jaws of the blacksmith's vise.

*Step by step*

113

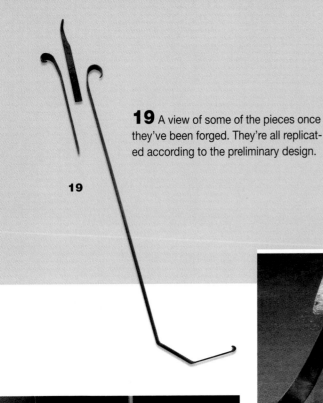

**19** A view of some of the pieces once they've been forged. They're all replicated according to the preliminary design.

**19**

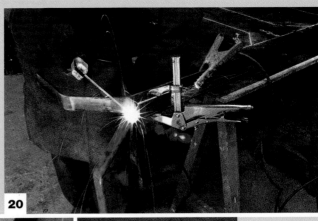

**20**

**21**

**22**

**23**

**20** The longest straps are welded to a piece of square tubing the same width as the straps to create two sets of strapping that fit together to make up the coat stand.

**21** A picture of the upper end of the coat stand where the joining method for the different pieces is visible.

**22** Join the two sets of straps together with a pin that passes through them. Weld the ends of the pin to the straps, and polish the weld to hide the welding beads.

**23** To finish up, go over all the welds with an angle grinder and a deburring disk. Note how the base is constructed to create greater stability and prevent wobbling.

*Flat enamel paint was used to finish the coat stand.*

# tricycle
# stool

In this exercise we will make a stool with three legs. We begin with a stone in a shape reminiscent of a bicycle seat. The stool will resemble a tricycle with three spirals of different sizes that will be welded together using coated rod. We will also make a structure for holding the stone seat to the rod assembly.

**1** and **2** Make a couple of preliminary sketches for planning purposes.

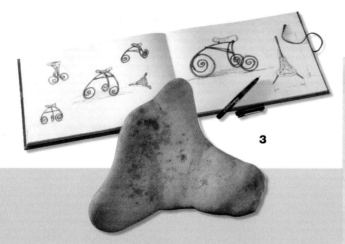

**3** Make the saddle-shaped stone the main focus of the piece.

**4** Draw a grid onto a copy of the original so that it can be enlarged to actual size without distorting the scale.

**5**

**5** Draw a grid on a flat surface, using the same number of equal squares as in the drawing.

**6**

**6** Transfer the shape by drawing freehand with chalk, keeping in mind the relationship between the grid and the original drawing.

**7** During the transfer of the shape, we noticed that the enlargement was too large for the stone, so we decided to reduce the size of the grid to remedy the problem.

**7**

**8**

**8** Use a piece of rope to go over the spiral and indicate how long the rod needs to be; the end is marked with a piece of chalk.

9

**9** The steel rod is measured with the rope. The distance is marked with a piece of chalk at the point where it will be cut.

**10** Start the spiral by heating the end of the rod and hammering it on the face of the anvil.

10

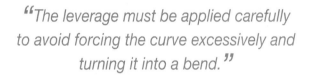

*"The leverage must be applied carefully to avoid forcing the curve excessively and turning it into a bend."*

11

**11** Once the spiral is started, apply some leverage to it in a bending tool clamped between the jaws of the blacksmith's vise. The leverage must be applied carefully to avoid forcing the curve excessively and turning it into a bend.

**12** Continue to check the shape of the spiral against the drawing as you proceed to curve the spiral. Try to use the drawing as a guide, but without copying it exactly.

12

**13**

**14**

**13** Join the three completed spirals by welding a straight piece of rod of the same diameter with coated rod.

**14** Curve a square rod by hammering it cold on a piece of U-shaped angle iron. This rod will serve to consolidate the spirals.

**15** With the curved rod placed on the ends of the spirals, mark with chalk the places where it will be bent.

**16** Use a torch to heat the spot where the bend will be made. Use a bending tool as a lever while the metal is heated.

**15**

**17**

**16**

**17** Place the now triangle-shaped rod on the ends of the three spirals, and weld in place. Wear protection against the intense light and potential burns from the arc welding.

*Step by step*

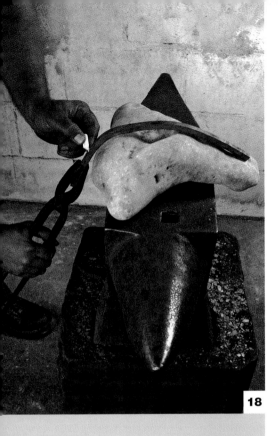

**18** Finally, construct the frame to hold up the stone seat. Heat a piece of square rod, and bend it to follow the shape of the stone. With a piece of chalk, mark the point where the excess rod is to be cut.

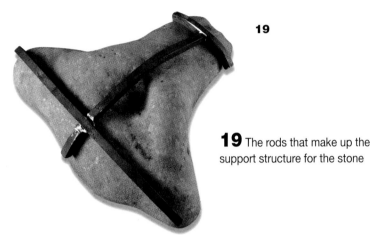

19

**19** The rods that make up the support structure for the stone

**20** Detail view of the joint in the support rods. Next, fill the hollows in the intersection between the rods with weld.

**21** Set the support for the stone in place, and weld it to the part where the spirals are connected.

*Stool in the shape of a tricycle with the stone in place. The finish was produced using a solution of water and salt, topped off with two coats of clear varnish.*

# serpentine shape
# weathervane

The following exercise will demonstrate how to make a weathervane. Keep in mind the concept of the weathervane as an object for the wind with the back part of it fashioned like a flag flapping in the wind. A special bending tool needs to be made, along with a template from thin wire that will serve as a guide in making the undulating shape. The tail will be forged from sheet steel about .040" (1 mm) thick. The pivot for the weathervane is composed of an axis with a pointed end on which the center of the arrow pivots.

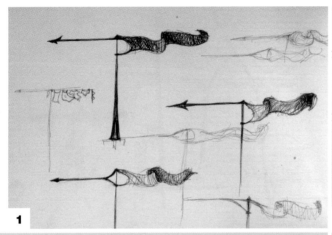

1

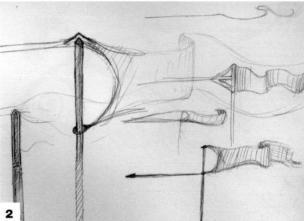

3

2

**1** Initial sketches of the weathervane, in which several possibilities for the position of the arrow are considered; each one retains the idea of a cloth flapping in the wind.

**2** Sketches are also made to work out the support system and pivot for the body of the weathervane.

**3** Similarly, preliminary sketches provide a study of how to secure the axis of the weathervane to the wood post where it will be located.

**4** A thin steel rod is bent with a bending tool to model the approximate wavy shape for the rear of the arrow.

**5** Once the curve is created, cut off the rest of the rod.

**6** Bend a round steel bar to create a special bending tool that will make it possible to impart a curve to the entire width of the sheet stock. Because of its thickness, use a pipe to extend the lever and exert more force.

**7** The finished bending tool. The long legs make it possible to curve the whole width of sheet stock for the back part of the weathervane arrow.

**8** Heat the end of the sheet steel, and bend it by prying it in the bending tool you made in step 6.

**9** Periodically to check the shape against the template.

**10** Proceed very cautiously when heating a sheet that's only about ⅟25 inch (1 mm) thick; it can easily reach high temperatures, and parts of the sheet may melt.

**11** Continue working the sheet in the tool made for this project.

**12** To finish up, forge the end that will be connected to the front of the arrow by hammering it on the rounded beak of the anvil. The rest of the forged steel sheet is cooled in water so it can be handled.

**13**

*"The rest of the forged steel sheet is cooled in water so it can be handled."*

**13** To forge the arrow itself, make a tenon by hammering the end of a round rod on the edge of the anvil face.

**14** Upset the tip a bit to thicken it so that the metal can be expanded to create the point of the arrow.

**15** Reheat the upset end, and simultaneously hammer it out and taper it to create the point.

**14**

**15**

**16**

**16** The shape of the arrow is worked cold with a triangular file. It helps to clamp the rod securely in the blacksmith's vise so that you can bear down as you file.

*Step by step*

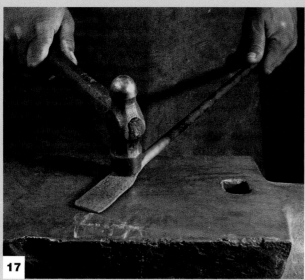

**17** Heat the opposite end of the arrow and hammer it flat on the face of the anvil.

**18** Shape the edges by turning the arrow as you hammer it out.

**19** Place the heated rod over the round hole in the anvil face. Hit it with a pointed steel rod and a hammer to force the heated part into the hole in the anvil.

**20** Next, make a slight twist by turning the flattened end with a bending tool. This turn will subsequently be used to connect the arrow to the forged sheet made in previous steps.

*"This turn will subsequently be used to connect the arrow to the forged sheet made in previous steps."*

**21**

**22**

**21** Connect the arrow to the undulating sheet steel by arc welding. Protect yourself from the radiation and ultraviolet rays that this type of welding produces.

**22** A close-up view of the joint between the two parts of the weathervane.

**23** and **24** Forge a ring that will stabilize the weathervane when it pivots on the main axis.

**23**

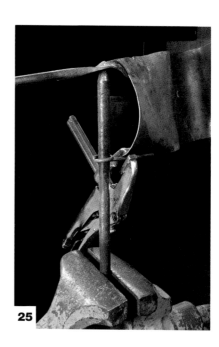

**25**

**24**

**25** A detail of the pivoting system for the weathervane clearly shows the twist and the indentation made in the hammered-out end of the arrow. Note the location of the ring for stabilizing the weathervane.

*Step by step*

**26**

**27**

**26** Taper and round a square rod to forge the axis on which the weathervane will pivot.

**27** After the end is forged, harden it to reduce the friction created by the rubbing of the weathervane on the axis.

**28**

**28** Polish the rounded part that will be subjected to friction to make it easier for the device to pivot in the wind.

**29**

**30**

**29** Forge the pieces for attaching the main axis to the wood post, and bend them to the proper dimensions.

**30** A view of how the axis of the weathervane is attached to the wood post

*The weathervane mounted on the wood post*

# *Diàspora*: a monumental **forging**

We will now show how a monumental sculpture, *Diàspora*, by the Spanish sculptor Ernest Altés, was forged. It was displayed in Copons (Barcelona, Spain) as an homage to the mule drivers of the Anoia region, who used to bustle along the roads of the Iberian peninsula. The industrial techniques—at Irizar Forging in Lazkao—are essentially the same as those demonstrated in this book. They vary only in scale. The material is laminated steel, but the hammer is a hydraulic press, the forge is a gas furnace, and the tongs, on a different scale, are activated from a crane.

**1** and **2** Start with sketches and drawings that will guide the development of the idea. Some drawings lead to others, and then it's time to put the idea into material form.

**3** Forge the piece to scale in the workshop forge, keeping in mind that the thickness of the sheet steel used and the various dimensions of the piece will be reproduced based on the selected scale.

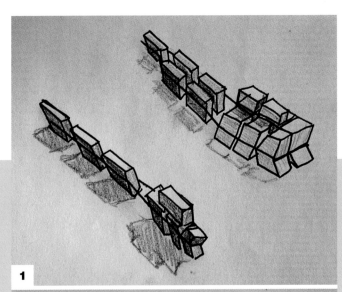

1

2

3

**4** In the industrial forge, begin with putting a U-shaped, cold-bent sheet into the gas furnace for heating. When pressure is applied to bend it, a couple of steel bars welded to the ends of the U maintain the shape.

**5** The heated piece is taken out using huge mechanical tongs activated from a crane by an operator.

**6** The piece is placed into the hydraulic press so that the area to be bent is close to the piston that will apply the pressure. Two pieces of steel placed on the floor immediately under the U-shaped piece facilitate the bending when the press exerts force onto the heated piece.

**7** Detail of the piston of the hydraulic press that will apply the pressure to the heated piece. The rounded end that starts with the beads of weld was created specifically for making this project. A small triangle of steel welded to each side of the piston makes it possible to create the fold when the pressure is applied.

Step by step

131

**8** The point at which pressure is applied to create the bend.

**9** This photo clearly shows the steel rods welded to the end of the U-shape to preserve the form during the bending process.

**10** Check the angle of the bend with a template made from sheet steel compared to the angle in the model.

**11** Put the piece back into the press to finish bending it to the correct angle.

**12** Just as in traditional blacksmithing, the piece is heated as many times as necessary.

**13** Cooling part of the piece with water during the forging process will keep it from distorting unnecessarily under pressure.

**14** Place the bent piece again into the press and line it up with the piston. Apply pressure until the desired shape is produced.

**15** Apply localized heatings with an oxyacetylene torch to finish up the forging. This repairs the small distortions that result from manipulating such a large piece.

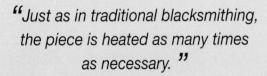

*"Just as in traditional blacksmithing, the piece is heated as many times as necessary."*

**16**

**17**

**18**

**16** The final appearance of one part of the work after the forging process is complete.

**17** The sculpture divided into three pieces, two with forged bends, and one, the piece in the middle, by bending cold.

**18** Check the dimensions before connecting the three parts that make up the work. Note the scale by comparing the artist, Ernest Altés, with the forged pieces.

*The assembled sculpture Diàspora (2004) in Copons in the Catalan region of Spain. It is made from pieces of forged steel and two sets of calcareous stones from various places in Catalonia. It's held together by a twisted steel cable.*

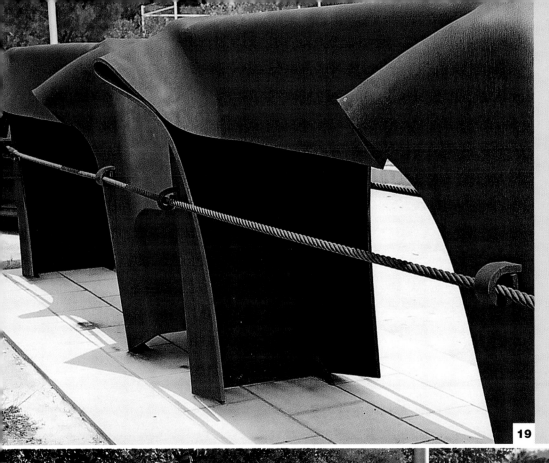

**19** Close-up views of the forged bends once the work was installed on a public road. In applying the finish, the metal was sandblasted to remove forging marks and to even out the natural rusting. The rings were welded on, and the cable passes through them and secures the sculpture to the ground.

19

**Gallery**

Ernest Altés, *Ofrena*, 1995.
Stone and forged steel,
4 x 6¼ x 6½ inches (10 x 16 x 17 cm)

Ares, *Xamán*, 1996. Forged and welded steel,
16¾ x 5½ x 4¾ inches (43 x 14 x 12 cm)

Katherine Gili, *Bitter Joy*, 2005.
Forged and welded steel,
58½ inches (150 cm) tall

Eduardo Chillida, *Peine del viento*, 1976. Eduardo Chillida Walk (Donosti-San Sebastian, Spain)

Anonymous, Door Knocker, 16th century. Forged steel (inv. No. 31565), Cau Ferrat Museum (Sitges, Spain)

Anonymous, Grate, 20th century. Forged steel. Center of Marakesh (Morocco)

Ares, *Record per a un cap d'onada*, 2005.
Oxy-cut and forged steel,
14¾ x 11¾ x 12½ inches (38 x 30 x 32 cm)

Ares, *Natura II*, 2003. Forged steel, 36¼ x 19 x 1¾ inches (93 x 49 x 4.5 cm)

Anonymous, Door Knocker, 19th century.
Steel. Old center of Santiagomillas
(León, Spain)

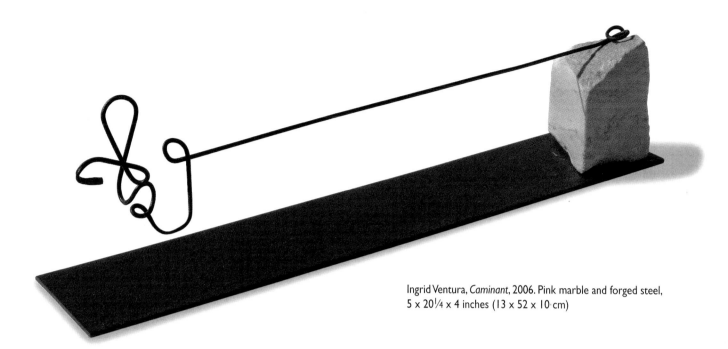

Ingrid Ventura, *Caminant*, 2006. Pink marble and forged steel,
5 x 20¼ x 4 inches (13 x 52 x 10 cm)

Ernest Altés, *Ch'i II*, 1995.
Basalt and forged stainless steel,
11 x 8 x 11 inches (28 x 21 x 28 cm)

Antonio Sobrino and Mercedes Cano,
*Bosque*, 2003. Forged steel.
Variable dimensions. Museum of Steel
(Oropesa de Mar, Spain)

Francisco Gazitua, *Huaso*, 2003. Forged steel,
11¾ x 11¾ inches (30 x 30 cm). Private collection

Anonymous, Shears.
Forged steel,
11¾ inches (30 cm) long.
Sonora Desert (Mexico)

Anonymous, Balance, 20th century. Forged steel,
15½ inches (40 cm) long, La Cerdaña
(Catalonia, Spain)

Antoni Gaudi, *Barandilla de la Pedrera*, 1906-1910. Forged steel. Casa
Milà a la Pedrera (Barcelona, Spain)

Ares, *Petita remor*, 2000.
Forged and oxy-cut steel,
6½ x 6¼ x 2¼ inches (17 x 16 x 6 cm)

Gemma López, *Cabró ibèric*, 1999.
Forged steel,
11¾ x 11¾ x 15½ inches (30 x 30 x 40 cm)

**B- Bead.** A deposit of metal that unites two pieces of metal in the welding process

**C- Cast iron.** An alloy composed of iron, carbon (in a proportion greater than 1.7%), and silicon, used for producing parts in molds

**Cold chisel.** A chisel for cutting hot or cold steel with the blow of a hammer

**Colophony rosin.** A residual product from the distillation of essence of turpentine

**Contraction.** A reduction in volume that metals experience after expanding

**Corrosion.** A chemical reaction that involves the slow destruction of the metal through the action of external agents

**D- Double boiler.** A process in which moderate, continuous heat is applied with a burner to the contents of one container placed inside another that holds water

**Ductility.** A property of metals that makes it possible to stretch them without breaking

**E- Electric intensity.** The quantity of electrons that pass through a section of conductor in a unit of time

**Expansion.** An increase in the volume of a metal through the effect of heat

**F- Fusibility.** The temperature at which a metal turns to liquid through heat absorption

**Fusion.** The passage of a body in solid state to liquid through the effect of heat

**Glossary**

**Fusion bath.** In welding, the space where the heat causes the added metal and the metal base to melt, forming a volume of material that produces the welding bead when it cools.

**G- Gum lacquer.** A natural resin that is sold in the form of flakes

**H- Hardness.** The resistance of materials to wearing away through friction

**Heating.** The action of heating a metal in the fire of the forge or by some other means, such as a torch

**I- Iron.** A ferrous metal with a carbon content lower than 0.05%

**M- Malleability.** The ability of heated metal to change shape through hammering

**Manometer.** A valve for reducing the pressure of a compressed gas in a tank or a compressor to the optimum working pressure

**Mild steel.** A steel alloy containing little carbon; it is ideal for blacksmithing work, but it is not suited to heat treating such as hardening

**O- Oxidation.** A combination of metal and oxygen from the air that forms a layer of oxide

**P- Patina.** A fine layer of oxide deposited on the surface of metals

**Plumbago.** Powdered graphite used for creating artificial patinas

**S- Slag.** In welding, a material produced by the decomposition of the coating on coated rod. Its purpose is to protect the fusion bath and the weld from oxidation.

**Spot welding.** The action of joining two pieces of metal through welds at various points

**Steel.** An alloy made up basically of iron and carbon. The latter is included in a percentage between 0.05 and 1.7%

**Stainless steel.** An alloy of steel, chrome, and nickel, among other metals, that makes it particularly resistant to corrosion

**T- Tenon.** A protrusion in the shape of a piece of steel after drawing it out while hammering it at heat

**V- Vacuum voltage.** The voltage in the ground clamp and the electrode clamp when not welding

**Volute.** A spiral shape

# Acknowledgments

To Parramón Publishing for developing these collections filled with resources for the arts and crafts.

To the University of Barcelona for generously providing the space for carrying out these exercises.

To the editors María Fernanda Canal and Tomàs Ubach for their confidence and their patience with the author.

To Joan Soto, photographer, for his great professionalism, his suggestions, and his good humor.

To the sculptor Ernest Altés for his willingness and attention, and for the use of the photographs from the creation of his work *Diàspora*.

To Rafael Cuartiellas, shop master and artist, for his subtle lessons.

To the sculptors: Ernest Altés, Gemma López, Ingrid Ventura, Antonio Sobrino, Mercedes Cano, Katherine Gili, and Fernando Gazitua, for improving this book by contributing images of their own artistic works for the Gallery section.

To Valerià Cortés for invaluable help in the step-by-step project of the grate with volutes.

To Jordi Torras and Rubén Campo, shop masters, for their daily help with moving items and locating tools and various types of materials for doing the exercises.

To D. José Ares, from Valdespino de Somozo (León, Spain) for allowing me to photograph his iron work.

To my parents, Clavelina and José, for taking care of my girls as often as necessary while I was working on this book.

I especially want to thank Martha and our girls Ia and Ona (in the photo) for their help and their understanding while I was working on this book. It would not have been possible without their laughter.